Eucharistic Origins

The Alcuin Club, founded in 1897, exists to promote the study of Christian liturgy in general, and in particular the liturgies of the Anglican Communion. The Club has published over 150 books, studies and pamphlets. Recent volumes include *They Shaped Our Worship: Essays on Anglican Liturgists*, edited by Christopher Irvine (1998), and *Companion to Common Worship*, Vol. 1, edited by Paul Bradshaw (2001). In collaboration with SPCK, the Club published two Liturgy Guides, *Memorial Services* by Donald Gray, and *Art and Worship* by Anne Dawtry and Christopher Irvine. Members of the Club receive publications of the current year free and others at a reduced price.

The Club works in partnership with GROW in the publication of the Joint Liturgical Studies series, and is one of the sponsoring bodies of PRAXIS. The Chairman of the Club is the Revd Canon Donald Gray CBE. Information concerning the annual subscription, applications for membership and lists of publications is obtainable from the secretary, Mr Jack Ryding, 'Ty Nant', 6 Parc Bach, Trefnant, Denbighshire LL16 4YE, or by email from alcuinclub@waitrose.com.

Visit the Alcuin Club website at **www.alcuin.mcmail.com**

Eucharistic Origins

Paul F. Bradshaw

Alcuin Club Collections 80

To Jonathan and Sarah

First published in Great Britain in 2004 by
Society for Promoting Christian Knowledge
Holy Trinity Church
Marylebone Road
London NW1 4DU

British Library Cataloguing-in-Publication Data
A catalogue record for this book is available from the British Library

ISBN 0-281-05615-3

10 9 8 7 6 5 4 3 2 1

Designed and typeset by Kenneth Burnley, Wirral, Cheshire
Printed in Great Britain by Ashford Colour Press

Contents

Introduction

The fundamental thesis advanced by Gregory Dix in his classic work, *The Shape of the Liturgy* (London, 1945), was (a) that there was a very high degree of standardization in Christian practice everywhere from a very early date; (b) that the form of the eucharistic rite was at first modelled on what Dix described as the sevenfold shape of the Last Supper, which was then modified at a very early stage into a fourfold shape of taking, blessing, breaking the bread and sharing; (c) that the meal as such disappeared from the rite at this same stage to become a separate institution called the *agape*; and (d) that instead the Eucharist was appended to a morning service of the word inherited from the Jewish synagogue but transferred to Sunday. While Dix was not the first scholar to put forward some of these ideas, he was responsible for popularizing them through his writing, and the constant reiteration of his hypotheses by subsequent teachers of liturgy for more than half a century has – as with all such repetitions – led to them being regarded by many as established facts. So seductive has been the picture painted by Dix that it has tended to blind us to its shortcomings and thus mislead us all. I intend therefore to explore the basis on which his thesis is built, to expose its weaknesses and to suggest an alternative way of looking at the evidence that seems to have more credibility and leads to a very different vision of eucharistic origins.

For the truth is that there is no really firm evidence that primitive eucharistic practice ever did conform to the sevenfold shape of the Last Supper, whereas there are signs of the existence of early Christian ritual meals that do not seem to relate themselves to this event or to be patterned according to its model. Although some scholars have reacted to this problem by propounding the notion that two quite different types of Eucharist existed in primitive Christianity,[1] Dix and many other

---

1 On this, see further below, pp. 27–8.

scholars tended to deal with it largely by means of exclusion, either by ignoring altogether scraps of evidence that did not fit their theory or by relegating them to the sidelines, ascribing them to deviant and/or heretical groups which could not possibly tell us anything about 'mainstream' Christian practices. But a method that simply eliminates all possible contrary evidence from an argument is hardly likely to be sound. We need to start not from a conviction about how things must have been, and then assemble the evidence in such a way that it fits our thesis, but rather from the evidence itself and see where it leads.

What we will discover is that neither the theory of a single root to eucharistic practice nor the hypothesis of a twofold origin provides an adequate explanation for the diversity of the testimony to what early Christians did. On the contrary, their practice seems to have been shaped by three principal variables: (a) in its ritual pattern, whether bread precedes cup, or cup precedes bread, or both occur together, or even that there is no cup at all; (b) in the elements that are used, whether bread and wine, bread and water, or bread alone or with other foodstuffs; and (c) in the meanings assigned to the rite, particularly whether it is related to the sayings of Jesus about his body and blood or not. The possible combinations of these three variables result in some variety in early Christian ritual meals, which I shall try to outline.

Dix and others also assumed a high degree of continuity in very many aspects of 'mainstream' Christian thought and practice from the apostolic age down to the fourth century, an assumption driven at least as much by concerns for a traceable line of doctrinal orthodoxy as by the historical data itself. Scholars today, however, would tend to see a greater element of change and dislocation in that historical period. L. Michael White, for example, has criticized Dix for presenting a virtually seamless evolution from the physical arrangements for worship of the early house-church to those of the later basilica.[2] Hence, I will adopt a more critical approach to the ways in which eucharistic practices and theologies did gradually begin to move towards a more 'mainstream' norm, through an examination first of the witnesses of the second century, with a special focus on Justin Martyr, and then of sources from the third century. We shall see just how few those sources are and how relatively little they can really tell us about the theology and practices of the period, compared with the bold pictures of that age that were often painted by earlier scholars, lumping the scattered pieces together to produce a composite whole and filling the gaps with material only

---

2 *Building God's House in the Roman World: Architectural Adaptation Among Pagans, Jews, and Christians* (Baltimore, MD, 1990), pp. 15–17.

known to us for the first time from a century or more later. We shall also see signs that it appears to have been much later than most scholars have supposed that the Eucharist came to be celebrated outside the context of a meal, and also that the understanding of the bread and wine as the body and blood of Christ sacrificed for believers came to predominate. In place of the latter, some at first focused instead on the image of feeding on the life-giving *flesh* and blood of Jesus, while others passed on the tradition of his sayings about body and blood, though independently of the paschal context and interpretation given to them in the New Testament writings. Finally, I will turn my attention to the emergence of the classic pattern of eucharistic prayers and the transformation of eucharistic theology and practice in the fourth century, where again the assumption of a clear line of continuity from the Jewish grace after meals, the *Birkat ha-mazon*, down to the eucharistic prayers of this much later age will have to be seriously questioned.

As indicated at the beginning of this Introduction, the Dixian hypothesis implicitly assumed a high degree of standardization and hence a very centralized model of ecclesiastical authority disseminating liturgical instructions to the churches scattered throughout the ancient world, a model perhaps having more in common with both Roman Catholic and Protestant churches from the sixteenth century onwards than it does with the situation in early or even medieval Christianity. Yet, it is not so surprising that earlier scholars did tend to think in this way about the early Church, because Jewish scholars too tended to view the history of their own liturgy in the same way, and if there was one thing that influenced Dix's approach it was that Christian liturgy was essentially built upon the foundations of Jewish liturgy. Recent decades, however, have seen very significant changes in Jewish scholarship, with the majority abandoning belief in a fixed and uniform – and hence centrally controlled – Jewish liturgy at the time of Jesus. Instead, most scholars would now see this situation emerging only very slowly over many centuries afterwards and in fact never fully achieved.[3] Similarly, modern New Testament scholarship tends to view nascent Christianity as an essentially pluriform movement with diverse theologies and diverse practices. Against such a background, therefore, the expectation of variety in Christian liturgical custom would seem more probable than

---

3 See for example Richard S. Sarason, 'On the Use of Method in the Modern Study of Jewish Liturgy', in W. S. Green (ed.), *Approaches to Ancient Judaism: Theory and Practice* (Missoula, MT, 1978), pp. 97–172 = Jacob Neusner (ed.), *The Study of Ancient Judaism* I (New York, 1981), pp. 107–79; Stefan C. Reif, *Judaism and Hebrew Prayer: New Perspectives on Jewish Liturgical History* (Cambridge, 1993).

that of uniformity, although it would be an equally erroneous method-ological error dogmatically to rule out a priori in every case the possibility of the latter as it was to eliminate the former from considera-tion.

My work here obviously draws upon the foundational material pre-sented in the second edition of my previous volume, *The Search for the Origins of Christian Worship* (London/New York, 2002), but in the early chapters it also builds to significant extent upon research already under-taken by Andrew McGowan, especially in his *Ascetic Eucharists* (Oxford, 1999), and I would like to acknowledge the considerable debt that I owe to him, as also to Maxwell Johnson, my colleague in the Theology Department at the University of Notre Dame, for reading this book in draft form and making helpful suggestions.

PAUL BRADSHAW

Abbreviations

AIR	E. J. Yarnold, *The Awe-Inspiring Rites of Initiation* (Slough, 1971; 2nd edn, Edinburgh/Collegeville, 1994).
CE	Common Era
EL	*Ephemerides Liturgicae*
EO	*Ecclesia Orans*
ET	English translation
HTR	*Harvard Theological Review*
JBL	*Journal of Biblical Literature*
JECS	*Journal of Early Christian Studies*
JEH	*Journal of Ecclesiastical History*
JTS	*Journal of Theological Studies*
OCP	*Orientalia Christiana Periodica*
RSR	*Revue des sciences religieuses*
SL	*Studia Liturgica*
SP	*Studia Patristica*
TS	*Theological Studies*
ZNW	*Zeitschrift für die neutestamentliche Wissenschaft*

All translations of primary sources, except where otherwise stated, are the work of the author, and full versions of abbreviated titles are given in the index of references.

Chapter 1

Last Supper and Institution Narratives

The Last Supper

The Christian tradition ascribes the origin of the Eucharist to Jesus' Last Supper with his disciples on the night before he died. It is important, however, to distinguish the Last Supper as an (alleged) historical event from the narratives of the Last Supper in the New Testament. Our only possible route to the former is through the latter, and hence some scholars have argued that while Jesus may indeed have held a final meal with his disciples, the narratives as we have them are creations of the early Church and so can tell us nothing about the actual historical roots of the Eucharist but can only witness to its later development.[1] On the other hand, there are other scholars who would accept that the accounts have certainly been influenced by the liturgical practices of the first Christians, but yet maintain that still discernible within them is a firm historical core.[2] However, because there are significant differences between the various accounts in the New Testament, they have been divided over which of them, if any, has best preserved the historical details. Joachim Jeremias, for example, opted for the Markan version of the interpretative words of Jesus over the bread and cup as coming

---

1 See, for example, Rudolf Bultmann, *Theology of the New Testament* (London/New York, 1952) I, pp. 144–51; Willi Marxsen, *The Lord's Supper as a Christological Problem* (Philadelphia, 1970); and more recently John Dominic Crossan, *The Historical Jesus: The Life of a Mediterranean Jewish Peasant* (Edinburgh/San Francisco, 1991), pp. 360–7.

2 Among recent examples, see E. P. Sanders, *The Historical Figure of Jesus* (Harmondsworth, 1993), pp. 263–4; John Meier, 'The Eucharist at the Last Supper; Did it Happen?', *Theology Digest* 42 (1995), pp. 335–51; John Koenig, *The Feast of the World's Redemption: Eucharistic Origins and Christian Mission* (Harrisburg, PA, 2000).

closest to the original,[3] Heinz Schürmann expressed a strong preference
for the Lukan narrative with its eschatological emphasis,[4] while Eduard
Schweizer considered the Pauline account the most primitive in form, in
spite of its more obvious liturgical character.[5] Subsequently, however,
Xavier Léon-Dufour, observing that both Jeremias and Schürmann
eventually abandoned their quest for *ipsissima verba* of Jesus, argued that
both older and newer elements are to be found in all the accounts,[6] a
point also made by John Meier in his defence of the historical roots of
the Last Supper tradition.[7]

The trend, therefore, in more recent scholarship has been to locate
the source of the Eucharist more broadly within the context of other
meals in Jesus' life and not merely the Last Supper, and largely following
the trajectory established by redaction-criticism, to take seriously
various layers of meaning that can be discerned within the New Testament and the different ways that the individual New Testament writers
describe those meals. Whereas earlier generations of scholars were concerned to try to find the common core behind the variety, scholars today
tend to be more interested in what the variety says about the particular
theologies of the Eucharist that were espoused by the individual writers
and their communities, even if they cannot always agree on the specific
layers of meaning that exist in the New Testament texts or on the special
emphasis being given to the material by a writer.[8]

---

3 *Die Abendmahlsworte Jesu* (Göttingen, 1935, 3rd edn 1960); ET = *The Eucharistic
Words of Jesus* (London/New York, 1966). Many other scholars followed him, including Rudolf Pesch, *Das Abendmahl und Jesu Todesverständnis* (Freiburg, 1978).

4 *Eine quellenkritische Untersuchung des lukanischen Abendmahlsberichtes Lk 22,
7–38*, published in 3 parts (Münster, 1953, 1955, 1957). A similar position was
adopted by Helmut Merklein, 'Erwägungen zur Überlieferungsgeschichte der
neutestamentlichen Abendmahlstraditionen', *Biblische Zeitschrift* 21 (1977), pp.
88–101, 235–44.

5 *The Lord's Supper according to the New Testament* (Philadelphia, 1967). See also
Paul Neuenzeit, *Das Herrenmahl. Studien zur paulinischen Eucharistieauffassung*
(Munich, 1960), pp. 103–20.

6 *Le Partage du pain eucharistique* (Paris, 1982); ET = *Sharing the Eucharistic Bread*
(New York, 1987), especially pp. 77ff., 96–8 and 157ff.

7 'The Eucharist at the Last Supper'.

8 See, for example, Léon-Dufour, *Sharing the Eucharistic Bread*, pp. 181–277;
Jerome Kodell, *The Eucharist in the New Testament* (Wilmington, DE, 1988), pp.
71–132; Bernd Kollman, *Ursprung und Gestalten der frühchristlichen Mahlfeier*
(Göttingen, 1990); Dennis E. Smith and Hal E. Taussig, *Many Tables: The Eucharist
in the New Testament and Liturgy Today* (London/Philadelphia, 1990), pp. 21–69;
Francis J. Moloney, *A Body Broken for a Broken People: Eucharist in the New Testament*
(Melbourne, Australia, 1990, 2nd edn Peabody, MA, 1997); Bruce Chilton, *A Feast
of Meanings: Eucharistic Theologies from Jesus through the Johannine Circle* (Leiden,

The New Testament narratives compared

The majority of modern New Testament scholars postulate that the narratives as we have them are the products of two early versions of the Last Supper tradition, one represented by the more Semitic style in Mark and Matthew and thought to stem from Jerusalem, and an Antiochene version found in the more Hellenistic form of Luke and Paul. Matthew not only reveals a general literary dependency on Mark but shares with him in particular the opening clause 'as they were eating', the parallelism of the sayings over the bread and cup ('this is my body . . . this is my blood') and the use of the verbs 'bless' over the bread and 'give thanks' over the cup. Matthew differs from Mark, however, in inserting the command 'eat' into the words over the bread and the command 'drink of it, all of you' to those over the cup, the latter replacing the statement in Mark that 'they all drank of it', and also in appending the phrase 'for forgiveness of sins' to the saying over the cup. In contrast, Paul and Luke do not have the opening phrase 'as they were eating' but instead separate the actions over the bread and the cup by the phrase 'after the supper'; they both use 'give thanks' instead of 'bless' over the bread as well as (at least by implication) over the cup; their sayings over bread and cup are asymmetrical ('body/new covenant in my blood'); and they alone mention the command to 'do this in my remembrance'.

However, the situation with regard to Luke's version of the narrative is complicated by a significant textual question. Although a large number of manuscripts of the Gospel contain the full text, there are some that have a shorter version, omitting everything after 'This is my body' in verses 19 and 20 (the portion enclosed in square brackets in our synoptic Table 1); and among the remaining manuscripts, there are other variants lying between these two extremes.[9] This means that the longer version has two cups, one over which Jesus gives thanks before taking the bread and one after, the imagery of the body and blood being applied to the bread and the second cup, while the shorter text omits the second cup entirely, and thus has the sequence 'cup–bread' with no 'blood' imagery being attached to the cup, a pattern similar to that of the *Didache* and possibly other sources, which I shall consider in later

---

1994); Eugene LaVerdiere, *The Eucharist in the New Testament and in the Early Church* (Collegeville, 1996); together with the critical comments in Andrew B. McGowan, 'The Meals of Jesus and the Meals of the Church: Eucharistic Origins and Admission to Communion', in Maxwell E. Johnson and L. Edward Phillips (eds), *Studia Liturgica Diversa: Essays in Honor of Paul F. Bradshaw* (Portland, OR, 2004), pp. 101–15.

9 For details, see Jeremias, *The Eucharistic Words of Jesus*, pp. 139–52.

Table 1: New Testament narratives of the Last Supper

Matthew 26	Mark 14	Luke 22	1 Corinthians 11
[20]When it was evening, he sat at table with the twelve; [21-25]and as they were eating, he said, 'Truly, I say to you . . . You have said so.'	[17]And when it was evening, he came with the twelve. [18-21]And as they were at table and eating, Jesus said, 'Truly, I say to you . . . not been born.'	[14]And when the hour came, he sat at table, and the apostles with him. [15-16]And he said to them, 'With desire I have desired . . . kingdom of God.' [17]And having accepted a cup, having given thanks, he said, 'Take this, and share it among you; [18]for I say to you, I shall not drink from now on from the fruit of the vine until the kingdom of God comes.'	[23]For I received from the Lord what I also delivered to you, that the Lord Jesus in the night when he was handed over
[26]Now as they were eating, Jesus, having taken bread and having blessed, broke (it), and giving (it) to the disciples, said, 'Take, eat; this is my body.' [27]And having taken a cup and having given thanks, he gave (it) to them, saying, 'Drink of it, all (of you); [28]for this is my blood of the [new] covenant, which (is) poured out for many for forgiveness of sins. [29]I say to you, henceforth I shall not drink again of this fruit of the vine until that day when I drink it new with you in my Father's kingdom.'	[22]And as they were eating, having taken bread, having blessed, he broke (it) and gave (it) to them and said, 'Take; this is my body.' [23]And having taken a cup, having given thanks, he gave (it) to them, and they all drank of it. [24]And he said to them, 'This is my blood of the [new] covenant, which (is) poured out for many. [25]Truly, I say to you, I shall not drink again of the fruit of the vine until that day when I drink it new in the kingdom of God.'	[19]And having taken bread, having given thanks, he broke (it) and gave (it) to them, saying, 'This is my body [which (is) given for you. Do this in my remembrance.' [20]And the cup likewise after the supper, saying, 'This cup (is) the new covenant in my blood, which (is) poured out for you'].	took bread, [24]and having given thanks, he broke (it), and said, 'This is my body which (is) [broken] for you. Do this in my remembrance.' [25]Likewise also the cup after the supper, saying, 'This cup is the new covenant in my blood. Do this, as often as you drink (it), in my remembrance.' [26]For as often as you eat this bread and drink this cup, you proclaim the Lord's death until he comes.

NB Square brackets indicate variant manuscript readings; round brackets words that need to be supplied for the sake of sense.

chapters. Although at first critical scholarship tended to prefer the shorter text as the original, in the course of the twentieth century the weight of scholarly opinion swung in favour of regarding the longer form as authentic, chiefly because of the strong manuscript support for it.

On the other hand, such a position still leaves unanswered the question as to why the shorter text should exist at all. Jeremias' hypothesis, that the deletion was made in order to protect the Eucharist from profanation,[10] will not really stand up to scrutiny. As Andrew McGowan has observed, why then would the words over the bread have not also been deleted?[11] Similarly, the suggestion that it was done to avoid having two cups[12] does not explain why the final words over the bread were also left out. Accidental omission can never be entirely ruled out, but seems improbable in the case of such a large unit, especially if it then resulted in a reading that was glaringly different from the story that was presumably familiar to the copyist. Is it not as least as likely that some copyists, faced with what was for them an unusual short version, would have felt the need to correct it by appending to varying extents missing elements, largely drawn from 1 Corinthians, to produce the various longer versions found in most manuscripts? If this were true, it would effectively eliminate from the original the features that Luke and Paul share in common and require us to view the account in Luke as a distinct third version of the tradition. But how might such an account have arisen? Recent New Testament scholars have refused to contemplate this solution to the problem because they have presumed that a ritual meal with the order cup first and then bread would have been an anomaly in primitive Christianity.[13] However, if – as I shall attempt to show in later chapters – just such an order was one of the ritual patterns well known to the first generations of believers, it becomes more credible that someone – especially someone in a Gentile environment unfamiliar with Passover meals – might have told the Last Supper story in this way so that it more accurately reflected the contemporary practice of their community.

---

10 Ibid., pp. 156–9.
11 '"First regarding the Cup . . .": Papias and the Diversity of Early Eucharistic Practice', *JTS* 46 (1995), pp. 551–5, here at p. 552.
12 See Schweizer, *The Lord's Supper according to the New Testament*, p. 19.
13 Jeremias, *The Eucharistic Words of Jesus*, p. 157, summarily dismissed the possibility: 'such a Lord's supper has never happened'.

A double strand in the tradition

Alongside the view that the various narratives reflect two discrete versions of the Last Supper tradition, there has also long been widespread acknowledgement among New Testament scholars of the existence of what R. H. Fuller called a 'double strand' within that tradition: on the one hand an eschatological focus, represented chiefly by the statement, 'I shall not drink of the fruit of the vine . . .',[14] in the three Gospel texts, and on the other hand the interpretative words over the bread and cup relating them to Jesus' body and blood.[15] While there might still be disagreement as to whether or not the interpretative words go back to the historical Last Supper, these scholars seem to share a general consensus that they would already have been combined with the eschatological theme in the eucharistic practice of the Palestinian Christian communities prior to Pauline influence.[16]

Léon-Dufour, however, has proposed that the two strands were transmitted through two distinct literary genres and implies that their combination was actually the work of the evangelists themselves, although he does not develop the consequences of this latter thesis. He believes that there was what he described as a 'cultic' tradition about the Last Supper, which belonged to the genre of the 'liturgical account', and a non-cultic or 'testamentary' tradition, which belonged to the genre of the 'farewell discourse'.[17] While some of the details of his analysis may be less than sure, he does appear to be on the right lines in distinguishing a narrative tradition in the three Gospels of a Passover meal incorporating an eschatological saying (or sayings) over a cup from an originally separate tradition of interpretative sayings of Jesus linked to actions over bread and cup that associated them with his body and blood. Many earlier scholars had recognized that the institution narratives did constitute a distinct source within the Gospels[18] – indeed, as we shall see later in this chapter, they had believed that the accounts were

---

14 Although described by some New Testament scholars as a 'vow of abstinence', Joseph A. Fitzmyer, *The Gospel according to Luke, X–XXIV* (Garden City, NY, 1985), p. 1396, rightly rejects that interpretation and calls it instead 'an emphatic statement of fact about the future'.

15 'The Double Origin of the Eucharist', *Biblical Research* 8 (1963), pp. 60–72.

16 See, for example, A. J. B. Higgins, *The Lord's Supper in the New Testament* (London, 1952), pp. 56–63; Schweizer, *The Lord's Supper according to the New Testament*, p. 25.

17 *Sharing the Eucharistic Bread*, pp. 82ff.

18 See, for example, Jeremias, *The Eucharistic Words of Jesus*, pp. 97, 99–100 and 113.

already being recited as liturgical texts at eucharistic celebrations – but they had not divided up the material in quite the same way as Léon-Dufour and so had not seen the full consequences of this.

It is the material containing the interpretative sayings to which the name 'institution narrative' has been given by scholars, but in truth they contain very little narrative as such. While they may appear to be descriptions of an event, they lack the sort of detail surrounding other events recorded in the Gospels. For example, nothing is said in them about the reactions of the disciples to the words and actions of Jesus. It would perhaps be more accurate to describe them as a pair of linked sayings than as a narrative as such. In the clearest example of this type of material, Paul's account in 1 Corinthians 11, there is not even any reference to the context of the sayings other than 'on the night when he was handed over', and that the saying over the cup came 'after the supper'.

Of the four versions, Luke 22.7–38 provides the most fully developed form of the other type, the 'farewell discourse'. Here the evangelist appears simply to have inserted verses 19–20 into this narrative as a block from the 'liturgical' tradition, resulting in two cups being mentioned and also in the apparently contradictory situation of Jesus declaring in verse 18 that he will no longer drink of the fruit of the vine and then in verse 20 of his doing so. Mark, on the other hand, appears to have tried to weave the material from the 'liturgical' tradition into his Supper narrative more carefully. His core narrative is not only shorter but also follows a different order: it begins with a discussion about betrayal (14.18–21, the parallel to which in Luke, 22.21–23, comes later, after the eschatological statement), and then the giving of the cup and his version of the eschatological statement follow, in that order, so that Jesus only declares that he will not drink wine again once they have all imbibed. Mark inserted the first half of the pair of interpretative sayings, concerning the bread (verse 22), before the reference to the cup that was already in the narrative, and combined the saying about the blood with the eschatological saying over the cup in verses 24–25. This results in the repetition of 'as they were eating' (verses 18 and 22) and also of the cup being drunk before the interpretative words are said, which Matthew adjusts by converting the narrative statement 'they all drank of it' into the command, 'Drink of it, all of you'.

This thesis concerning the development of the Gospel texts may perhaps be grasped more clearly if we now present the relevant portions of Mark and Luke with the apparently inserted 'liturgical' material indicated by the use of italics:

Mark 14	*Luke 22*
[17]And when it was evening, he came with the twelve. [18]And as they were at table eating, Jesus said, 'Truly, I say to you that one of you will betray me, one eating with me.' [19]They began to be sorrowful and to say to him one by one, 'Is it I?' [20]He said to them, '(It is) one of the twelve, one dipping with me in the dish.' [21]For the Son of man goes as it is written concerning him, but woe to that man by whom the Son of man is betrayed. (It would have been) good for him if that man had not been born.' [22]*And as they were eating, having taken bread, having blessed, he broke (it) and gave (it) to them and said, 'Take; this is my body.'*[23]And having taken a cup, having given thanks, he gave (it) to them, and they all drank from it. [24]And he said to them, '*This is my blood of the [new] covenant, which (is) poured out for many.* [25]Truly, I say to you, I shall not drink again of the fruit of the vine until that day when I drink it new in the kingdom of God.'	[14]And when the hour came, he sat at table, and the apostles with him. [15]And he said to them, 'With desire I have desired to eat this Passover with you before I suffer, [16]for I say to you, I shall not/never again eat it until it is fulfilled in the kingdom of God.' [17]And having accepted a cup, having given thanks, he said, 'Take this, and share it among you; [18]for I say to you, I shall not drink from now on from the fruit of the vine until the kingdom of God comes.' [19]*And having taken bread, having given thanks, he broke (it) and gave (it) to them, saying, 'This is my body [which (is) given for you. Do this in my remembrance.'*[20]*And the cup likewise after the supper, saying, 'This cup (is) the new covenant in my blood, which (is) poured out for you].* [21]But behold the hand of the one betraying me (is) with me on the table. For the Son of man goes according to what has been determined, but woe to that man by whom he is betrayed.' [22]And they began to question one another, which of them. . . .

Although Léon-Dufour appears unaware of it, this explanation also provides a solution to the unusual 'mixed' usage of 'bless' over the bread but 'give thanks' over the cup in Mark and Matthew. In spite of a persisting misconception among many New Testament scholars that these verbs are merely synonyms that might be employed interchangeably,[19]

---

19 See, for example, Geoffrey W. Bromiley (ed.), *The Theological Dictionary of the New Testament* 9 (Grand Rapids, MI, 1974), p. 411; and below, p. 34.

they actually refer to two quite different Jewish liturgical constructions: the *berakah*, 'blessing', which used the passive participle of the verb *barak*, 'Blessed are you . . . who . . .', and which eventually became normative in later Jewish prayer; and the *hodayah*, 'thanksgiving', which used an active form of the verb *hodeh*, 'I/we give thanks to you . . . because . . .'.[20] Both of the forms were in use by Jews in the first century, although the Qumran material[21] and also Hellenistic Jewish sources[22] seem to display a preference for the latter over the former. One might well have expected that a tradition that employed a *berakah* over the bread would have done the same over the cup, just as the Lukan/Pauline version from a Hellenistic background appears to have used a thanksgiving for both.[23] However, if Mark were grafting his 'liturgical' material on to a source where 'thank' was already in use for the eschatological saying over the cup, it would account for his retention of that verb in relation to the annexed cup-saying while at the same time he added the full unit concerning the bread, including the verb 'bless', from that tradition.

But how does the explanation of a twofold source for the Supper material affect the earlier suggestion that the shorter text of Luke might be the original? At first sight, it might seem unlikely that the evangelist would merely have added the interpretative saying over the bread and not that over the cup from the 'liturgical' tradition. However, if we set aside the assumption that Luke must already have been familiar with an institution narrative of the kind quoted by St Paul and with a eucharistic practice that employed bread and wine and related them to the body and blood of Christ, the picture may become a little more credible. As I shall suggest in Chapter 3, the evangelist may instead have been acquainted with a eucharistic pattern of a 'bread only' kind and lacking any specific reference to the Last Supper, and hence Mark's Gospel text may have been the only source known to him that identified bread and wine with the body and blood. It is conceivable, therefore, that he might have chosen simply to add the saying over the bread from Mark,

---

20 See further Paul F. Bradshaw, *Daily Prayer in the Early Church* (London, 1981/New York, 1982), pp. 11–16; idem, *The Search for the Origins of Christian Worship*, pp. 43–4.

21 See, for example, Florentino García Martínez, *The Dead Sea Scrolls Translated* (2nd edn, Leiden, 1996), pp. 317–70.

22 See, for example, Jean Laporte, *La doctrine eucharistique chez Philon d'Alexandrie* (Paris, 1972), pp. 82–4; ET = *Eucharistia in Philo* (New York, 1983), pp. 53–5.

23 Note, however, that in two other meal contexts Luke employs 'bless' rather than 'give thanks' (Luke 9.16; 24.30), although using 'give thanks' in Acts 27.35.

changing the verb 'bless' to the more familiar 'give thanks' as he did so.[24] The omission of a further cup-saying after the bread would also obviate the situation in which Jesus, having stated that he would not drink wine again, then immediately does so.[25]

As was noted above, there has been a general consensus among New Testament scholars that the two strands of the Last Supper tradition were combined very early. Yet, if the evangelists were still making somewhat clumsy attempts to conflate the two sets of sayings as they composed the Gospels, it would seem very unlikely that they had already been integrated in earlier Christian history. This suggests that in the second half of the first century there were Christian communities that still did not connect the tradition of the sayings of Jesus about his body and blood over bread and cup directly with a Passover meal at which he made an eschatological statement but at most only with 'the night when he was handed over', just as St Paul – and presumably the community from which he inherited his tradition – did. It is equally probable that there were other Christian communities that knew nothing of that particular tradition but may have been aware only of stories that Jesus celebrated the Passover with his disciples and engaged in discourse with them, including making eschatological statements, all of which had no direct effect in shaping the pattern of their regular ritual meals together beyond a heightened expectation of his imminent return.[26] This explains why there are in the New Testament both Passover elements in relation to the Last Supper and also other elements that seem irreconcilable with that: they belong to quite different strands of the tradition. The various attempts that have been made by modern scholars to harmonize the texts are thus attempting the impossible.[27]

---

24 The suggestion that Luke simply added Mark's saying over the bread to his Passover material has already been by made others: see Henry Chadwick, 'The Shorter Text of Luke xxii 15–20', *HTR* 50 (1957), pp. 249–58; B. P. Robinson, 'The Place of the Emmaus Story in Luke-Acts', *New Testament Studies* 30 (1984), pp. 481–97, esp. pp. 488–90.

25 The contention of Jeremias and others that Jesus himself did not drink even from the first cup seems unwarranted: see *The Eucharistic Words of Jesus*, pp. 208–9. Fitzmyer, *The Gospel according to Luke*, p. 1398, concludes that 'it is impossible to say whether Jesus himself tasted it first'.

26 On the other hand, it is possible that the tradition of Jesus' eschatological saying did have some influence in shaping their annual celebration of Easter, as early Christians fasted during the Jewish Passover and only broke that fast and celebrated the Eucharist at cockcrow: see Jeremias, *The Eucharistic Words of Jesus*, pp. 216–18; Thomas J. Talley, *The Origins of the Liturgical Year* (New York, 1986), pp. 5–7.

27 For these, see Bradshaw, *The Search for the Origins of Christian Worship*, pp. 63–5.

The function of the narratives

In common with many scholars, I have been describing the second Last Supper tradition as 'liturgical'. But just what does that mean? On the one hand, there has been a widespread predilection among New Testament scholars to assume that the narratives were already in use as liturgical texts by first-generation Christians before the Gospels themselves (and even 1 Corinthians) were composed, that is, that they were regularly recited at the community's eucharistic celebrations. Thus, Jerome Murphy-O'Connor expresses a typical point of view when he says:

> It is now generally recognized that these four accounts are derived from liturgical versions. What Jesus actually said and did was preserved with minor variations in different churches, and when the gospels were given their definitive form the words actually in use in the various eucharistic celebrations were inserted into the narrative of the Last Supper.[28]

Such scholars have reached this judgement principally on the basis of the particular stylistic and verbal characteristics of the narratives, but as Louis Ligier has pointed out, 'we lack any means of distinguishing in the New Testament between a liturgical tradition and a purely gospel tradition. The institution narratives are unique of their kind: we have no point of comparison.'[29]

By contrast, there has been a growing conviction in recent decades among liturgical scholars, on the other hand, that the narratives were not so used, chiefly because there is a complete absence of evidence for them being employed in this way until several centuries later, when they appear to be innovations in eucharistic prayers rather than the continuation of an ancient tradition.[30] What these scholars have generally done,

---

28 'Eucharist and Community in First Corinthians', in R. Kevin Seasoltz (ed.), *Living Bread, Saving Cup* (Collegeville, 1982), pp. 1–30, here at p. 17. See the long list of those holding a similar opinion in Schürmann, *Eine quellenkritische Untersuchung*, part 2, p. 144, n. 475.

29 'The Origins of the Eucharistic Prayer: From the Last Supper to the Eucharist', *SL* 9 (1973), pp. 161–85, here at p. 163. See also the critique by Andrew B. McGowan: 'Is there a Liturgical Text in this Gospel? The Institution Narratives and Their Early Interpretive Communities', *JBL* 118 (1999), pp. 73–87.

30 See below, p. 140. The only major exception to this trend has been Cesare Giraudo, who believes that Christian eucharistic prayers were originally patterned after a Jewish *todah* prayer form with a bipartite structure of anamnesis–epiclesis,

therefore, has been to treat the narratives as functioning in effect as the pattern or script for the earliest Christian eucharistic celebration, an idea propounded by Felix L. Cirlot and popularized by Gregory Dix. Cirlot asserted that 'there seems, then, no good reason to doubt that the primitive Eucharist was a fairly exact replica of the Last Supper as we have pictured it . . .';[31] and Dix, although acknowledging that 'the last supper of our Lord with His disciples is the source of the liturgical eucharist, but not the model for its performance', did believe that later practice was based upon 'a somewhat drastic modification' of its pattern:

> The New Testament accounts of that supper as they stand in the received text present us with what may be called a 'seven-action scheme' of the rite then inaugurated. Our Lord (1) took bread; (2) 'gave thanks' over it; (3) broke it; (4) distributed it, saying certain words. Later He (5) took a cup; (6) 'gave thanks' over that; (7) handed it to His disciples, saying certain words. . . . With absolute unanimity the liturgical tradition reproduced these seven actions as four: (1) The offertory; bread and wine are 'taken' and placed on the table together. (2) The prayer; the president gives thanks to God over bread and wine together. (3) The fraction; the bread is broken. (4) The communion; the bread and wine are distributed together.[32]

The change from a sevenfold shape to a fourfold one Dix thought had probably taken place 'after the writing of I Cor. but before the writing of the first of our gospels', when the Eucharist was separated from the meal

---

together with an embolism in the middle which served as the *locus theologicus* for the entire formula, and that it was this embolism that eventually was transformed into the institution narrative: *La struttura letteraria della preghiera eucaristica* (Rome, 1981); idem, 'Irrepetibilità dell'evento fondatore e iterazione del rito: la mediazione del segno profetico. Prospettive teologiche sul rapporto tra Ultima cena, Morte-Risurrezione ed Eucaristia', *Rivista di teologia* 24 (1983), pp. 385–402; 'Le récit de l'institution dans la prière eucharistique a-t-il des précédents?', *Nouvelle revue théologique* 106 (1984), pp. 513–35. For criticism of the validity of Giraudo's thesis, see Paul F. Bradshaw, '*Zebah Todah* and the Origins of the Eucharist', *EO* 8 (1991), pp. 245–60; J. Briend in a review of Giraudo's book in *La Maison-Dieu* 181 (1990), pp. 155–9; and Albert Gerhards, 'Entstehung und Entwicklung des Eucharistischen Hochgebets im Spiegel der neueren Forschung. Der Beitrag der Liturgiewissenschaft zur liturgischen Erneuerung', in A. Heinz and H. Rennings (eds), *Gratias Agamus. Studien zum eucharistischen Hochgebet. Für Balthasar Fischer* (Fribourg, 1992), p. 80.
31 *The Early Eucharist* (London, 1939), p. 168; see also ibid., pp. 21–2.
32 *The Shape of the Liturgy*, p. 48. Dix (ibid., p. 58, n. 2) admitted owing a considerable debt for some of his ideas to Cirlot.

as such.[33] He reached this conclusion on the grounds that the Corinthians' misunderstanding of the nature of the Eucharist would only make sense if it were still integrated in the meal, and also because Matthew and Mark show themselves uninterested in the relation of the actions over bread and cup to the meal compared to the reference to 'after supper' in the Pauline account: 'They do not even state where and when in the meal they came, or whether together or at an interval.'[34]

But this idea must be questioned too. We do not possess one scrap of direct testimony that the earliest Christian Eucharist ever conformed itself to the model of the Last Supper, with a bread ritual before the meal and a cup ritual afterwards. It may of course have been the custom in some communities, but we have no actual evidence that it was. That is simply an inference that has been made from the narratives themselves. Nor is the hypothesis of an original sevenfold eucharistic pattern necessary in order to explain the existence of the so-called fourfold shape in later liturgies.[35] Moreover, even the text of Exodus 12 did not function as the definitive script for the ritual of the Jewish Passover meal at that time, although in its earlier history it probably had done so – and in subsequent centuries practice diverged still further from the text[36] – and this was a text that was not simply a narrative, as in the case of the Last Supper, but explicitly a set of instructions as to what to do. Why then should the early Christians have felt bound to follow in exact detail in their weekly community meals together the description of what Jesus had done at what was allegedly the special annual event of the Passover meal? Even those who thought that Jesus had said 'Do this in my remembrance' did not necessarily interpret this to mean, 'Do this, *in exactly the same order*, in my remembrance'. It is more likely that they understood the command to mean that whenever they ate a ritual meal together, whatever form it took, they were to eat and drink in remembrance of him. In 1 Corinthians the narrative is not functioning as ordo or script: Paul quotes it in order to remind the Corinthians of the meaning that he attaches to their celebration of the Lord's Supper – the proclamation of the Lord's death until he comes (1 Cor. 11.26) – and not of its ritual sequence.[37] And indeed, as we shall see later, there are

---

33 Ibid., p. 101.
34 Ibid., p. 98.
35 See below, p. 75.
36 See Joseph Tabory, 'Towards a History of the Paschal Meal', in Paul F. Bradshaw and Lawrence A. Hoffman (eds), *Passover and Easter: Origin and History to Modern Times* (Notre Dame, 1999), pp. 62–80.
37 Enrico Mazza, *The Origins of the Eucharistic Prayer* (Collegeville, 1995), p. 71, observes that Paul is not presenting the narrative of the Last Supper 'in order to give suggestions of a ritual kind'.

some signs that the actual order of their meal was in fact quite different from the pattern of the Last Supper.[38]

So what was the purpose of the narratives? Léon-Dufour is undoubtedly right to describe them as etiological stories,[39] but they are etiological stories intended to furnish an explanation of the basis for particular beliefs rather than of the origin of certain liturgical patterns. The remembrance of the sayings of Jesus over the bread and cup provided the grounds for the conviction that the bread and the contents of the cup consumed at Christian ritual meals were the body and blood of Christ. Thus, the institution narratives were neither liturgical texts to be recited at the celebration nor liturgical instructions to regulate it, but instead catechesis of a liturgical kind. It was their regular repetition for catechetical purposes within some – but apparently not all[40] – early Christian communities that gave them their particular literary style and character, and that has in turn misled New Testament scholars into imagining that they must therefore have been read as part of every celebration.

This verdict receives some confirmation from the use to which the institution narrative seems to have been put in the Christian literature of the next few centuries. Although citations are very sparse in the extant sources of this period, the particular forms in which the narrative appears show signs of the continuing existence of an oral tradition that was independent of the New Testament texts. The earliest versions are very brief, in contrast to the longer scriptural accounts and also to the much more prolix forms found in later liturgical texts. They lack any reference to the occasion and context in which the sayings of Jesus were uttered or to the ritual shape of the Last Supper, and even any of the interpretative phrases connecting body and blood to the covenant or giving sacrificial meaning to them, such as 'which is for you' or 'which is poured out for many for forgiveness of sins'. What tend to remain are simply the identification of the bread and cup with the body and blood of Christ and the dominical command to 'do this' in remembrance. In other words, these versions contain what I have suggested above was the 'sayings' material inserted into the accounts in the Synoptic Gospels, but in an even more basic form lacking the sacrificial expansions found there. This implies that this material continued to circulate separately even after the Gospels were composed, and suggests that the historical setting of the sayings or any close link with the death of Christ was not

---

38 See below, pp. 45ff.
39 *Sharing the Eucharistic Bread*, p. 83.
40 See further below, p. 60.

regarded as of importance in early traditions of eucharistic thought. Rather, as E. C. Ratcliff observed, 'in the liturgical tradition of Justin's time and of the period immediately after him the Lord's bread and cup . . . are conceived as existing in their own right, possessed of a significance which is peculiar to themselves, because conferred by the words of the Lord'.[41] This in turn seems to support the conclusion that the narrative functioned as a catechetical rather than a liturgical text as such, until at least the middle of the fourth century when it began to be inserted within eucharistic prayers themselves, and even that insertion was parenthetical and also appears to have been made for catechetical purposes.[42] I will therefore conclude this chapter by surveying the extant quotations during these early centuries.[43]

Justin Martyr

In his *First Apology* written in the middle of the second century at Rome, Justin Martyr summarized the Gospel narratives as follows: 'Jesus, having taken bread, having given thanks, said, 'Do this in my remembrance; this is my body'; and similarly having taken the cup and having given thanks, said, 'This is my blood'; and gave to them [the apostles] alone.'[44]

In comparison with the canonical versions, this account is very brief indeed. There is not even a reference to the breaking of the bread. As Ratcliff observed in his analysis of the text, it is composed almost entirely of a mixture of words and phrases that can be paralleled in the narratives of both Matthew and Luke, and he believed that it sounded like a formulary regularly used in catechesis rather than an ad hoc composition by Justin.[45] Since Justin elsewhere has many quotations that are

---

41 'The Eucharistic Institution Narrative of Justin Martyr's *First Apology*', *JEH* 22 (1971), pp. 97–102, here at p. 102 = A. H. Couratin and D. H. Tripp (eds), *E. C. Ratcliff: Liturgical Studies* (London, 1976), pp. 41–8, here at p. 46.
42 See below, p. 140. I am grateful to David Pitt, a student in the doctoral programme in liturgical studies at the University of Notre Dame, for first suggesting this idea to me.
43 For comparative analyses of versions of the institution narrative occurring in later eucharistic prayers, see Paul Cagin, *L'euchologue latine étudiée dans la tradition de ses formules et de ses formulaires* (Paris, 1912), pp. 224–51; F. Hamm, *Die liturgischen Einsetzungsberichte im Sinne vergleichender Liturgieforschung untersucht* (Münster, 1928).
44 *First Apology* 66.3. For the full context, see below, p. 62.
45 See above, n. 41. Ratcliff's further suggestion, that it might have been used liturgically at least on baptismal days, is simply speculation.

harmonizations of Matthew and Luke,[46] it could well be that he was drawing on an existing collection of such material. On the other hand, this quotation contains something that occurs in no other extant ancient version of the narrative: the placing of the command, 'Do this in my remembrance', first rather than last, before the words, 'this is my body'. This unusual order could be a consequence of the fact that Justin has introduced the narrative with the statement that the apostles 'have handed down what was commanded them', and so the notion of the command was uppermost in his mind. It should be noted, however, that the only canonical Gospel to contain the command at all is the longer text of Luke, and in the one place in his writings where it is certain that Justin is quoting that particular Gospel, it is the so-called Western Text that he knows, the text that contains the shorter version of the institution narrative lacking the command.[47]

Of course, even though Justin claims to be citing here what was handed down by 'the apostles in the records composed by them which are called gospels', it could be that he is simply giving an imperfect quotation from memory – something that he seems to do in other places – and actually drawing partially on 1 Corinthians 11.24. But given the crucial character of this particular narrative, that would be surprising. Whatever its origin, however, it is clear from the context that the reason for the quotation is to support Justin's preceding assertion that 'we have been taught that the food over which thanks have been given . . . is both the flesh and blood of that incarnate Jesus'. In other words, its role is doctrinal rather than strictly liturgical, intended to justify what is believed rather than the ritual pattern of what is done.[48] If, therefore, apart from the unusual order, it does faithfully reflect a regular catechetical formulary rather than an extract from a collection of harmonized Gospel sayings, it indicates the freedom with which the narrative might still be transmitted, and raises the possibility that the particular form here may be older than the adoption of written Gospel texts within Justin's community. Some support may also be lent to the idea that he was aware of an independent narrative tradition by his use of the word *homoios*, 'similarly', instead of the Lukan and Pauline equivalent, *hosautos*.[49]

---

46 On Justin's gospel traditions, see Helmut Koester, *Ancient Christian Gospels: Their History and Development* (London, 1990), pp. 360–402.
47 Ibid., p. 365.
48 On Justin's eucharistic theology, see below, p. 89.
49 On this, see also below, p. 90.

Irenaeus

As in the case of Justin, there is only one quotation of the whole institution narrative in the writings of Irenaeus at Lyons in the latter part of the second century: 'He took that created thing, bread, and gave thanks, saying, "This is my body." And the cup likewise, which is part of that creation to which we belong, he declared his blood . . .' (*Adv. haer.* 4.17.5). Again, like Justin, there is no reference to the context of the sayings, either to the impending passion or to the order of the Supper. The opening sequence 'took–gave thanks–saying' also resembles Justin, as does the omission of any reference to the breaking of the bread, thus hinting at the possibility that Irenaeus too may have been familiar with a standardized catechetical summary of the kind apparently known to Justin. Once again, the context in which it is used reveals its function to be doctrinal rather than liturgical: Irenaeus employs it to support his assertion that 'the Lord gave directions to his disciples to offer first-fruits to God from God's own creatures', in spite of the fact that his quotation itself does not include the explicit dominical command to repeat the action.[50]

Elsewhere, however, Irenaeus reveals that he is also familiar with at least one New Testament narrative of the Last Supper, quoting a part of the account directly from Matthew:

> when he had given thanks over the cup, and had drunk of it, and given it to the disciples, he said to them: 'Drink of it, all (of you): this is my blood of the new covenant, which will be poured out for many for forgiveness of sins. But I tell you, I will not drink henceforth of the fruit of this vine until that day when I will drink it new with you in my Father's kingdom.' (*Adv. haer.* 5.33.1)

We may note the use of the future tense here 'which will be poured out', a reading that recurs in a number of other renderings of the Matthean narrative, but also the description of Jesus drinking before giving the cup to the disciples or saying the words, something not otherwise found in Matthew.

North Africa: Tertullian and Cyprian

By the third century, however, the New Testament writings are beginning to influence the form in which the sayings of Jesus are cited, as those writings gain authority as Scripture. Although Tertullian does not

---

50 On Irenaeus' eucharistic theology, see below, p. 82.

quote the narrative in full, he does refer briefly to it in his treatise against Marcion at the end of the second century, and renders it quite freely. He does not mention either giving thanks or breaking the bread, and locates the giving before the interpretative words. On the other hand, he does situate it in its paschal context and refers to the covenant. 'Having taken bread and given it to the disciples, he made it his body by saying, "This is my body". . . . Similarly, when mentioning the cup and making the covenant to be sealed by his blood, he affirms the reality of his body.'[51] Tertullian's brevity and selectivity, therefore, may more probably be accounted for by his desire to combat the docetism of his opponent than by adherence to an independent catechetical tradition.

Certainly, when we come to our next witness, Cyprian, bishop of Carthage in the middle of the third century, we are in a quite different situation from the earlier narrative summaries. Cyprian quotes only part of the narrative of the Last Supper but his source is clearly a canonical Gospel, Matthew 26.27–28, rather than a separate catechetical tradition:

> For, on the eve of his passion, taking the cup, he blessed, and gave (it) to his disciples, saying, 'Drink of this, all (of you); for this is the blood of the covenant, which will be poured out for many for forgiveness of sins. I tell you, I shall not drink again of this fruit of the vine until that day when I shall drink new wine with you in my Father's kingdom.' (*Ep.* 63.9)

Although there is no trace of any influence from the other Gospels here, there are two interesting variations from the usually accepted Matthean text. Cyprian uses 'blessed', the word used by Matthew for the bread, rather than 'give thanks', used by both Mark and Matthew for the cup. He also uses the future tense 'will be poured out' rather than the present. The first of these variants also occurs in the institution narrative of the later Roman Canon. The second, as we have seen, appears in Irenaeus' citation of Matthew 26.28, and it is also used in the Old Latin translation of the Matthean passage. We may note also that when Cyprian then goes on a little later to quote 1 Corinthians 11.23b–26 in full (*Ep.* 63.10), he uses the future in connection with the bread, 'which will be given up (*tradetur*) for you', against the usual text which has simply 'which is for you', but partially echoing the Lukan text, 'which is given (*datur*) for you'.

---

51 *Adv. Marc.* 4.40.3. For Tertullian's eucharistic theology, see below, pp. 94ff.

The *Apostolic Tradition*

Although in its extant state the untitled and anonymous ancient church order known as the *Apostolic Tradition* and often (wrongly) attributed to Hippolytus of Rome dates from the fourth century or later,[52] yet that does not mean that the institution narrative which its eucharistic prayer contains may not have had an independent existence as a catechetical text long before it was incorporated into that prayer. It is of course difficult to know just how old the narrative itself might be, and where it might have originated, which does limit its value in helping to trace the evolution of the narrative tradition in early Christianity. The task is made even more difficult because it exists only in the Latin and Ethiopic versions of the church order:

Latin	*Ethiopic*
. . . taking bread, giving thanks to you, he said: 'Take, eat, this is my body which will be broken for you.' Likewise also the cup, saying: 'This is my blood which is poured out for you. When you do this, you do my remembrance.'	Then, having taken bread, he gave thanks and said: 'Take, eat; this is my body which will be broken for you.' And in the same way (with) the cup he said: 'This is my blood which will be poured out for you. When you do this, you make a memorial of me.'

This account is composed largely of words and phrases that are also found in different canonical accounts and so cannot be thought of as drawing on any one of them in particular. The sequence 'take–give thanks–said' in relation to the bread parallels Justin's opening, including both the absence of the conjunction 'and' and the omission of any explicit reference to the Supper and to the breaking of bread, but the form of the dominical words is different, a mixture of those found in Matthew ('Take, eat, this is my body') with those in some manuscripts of 1 Corinthians ('This is my body which is broken for you'), but without the latter's command to repeat the action. The use of the future tense 'will be broken' is unusual in early Christian citations of the words of Jesus, although we have encountered 'will be given up for you' in Cyprian's quotation of 1 Corinthians 11.24. Bernard Botte thought that

---

52 For the arguments, see Paul F. Bradshaw, Maxwell E. Johnson and L. Edward Phillips, *The Apostolic Tradition: A Commentary* (Minneapolis, 2002), pp. 1–6 and 13–15.

it was due to a misunderstanding of a present participle by the Latin and Ethiopic translators,[53] but it should be noted that the future tense (*confringetur*) does also occur in the institution narrative of the eucharistic prayer quoted by Ambrose of Milan in the fourth century (*De sacramentis* 4.21). The words over the cup offer no precise parallel with any one of the canonical accounts, although 'which is poured out for you' corresponds to what is found in the longer text of Luke, and the final command echoes 1 Corinthians 11.25. The use of the future in connection with the cup in the Ethiopic is probably simply the result of an attempt to make the two sayings parallel rather than an example of the tradition of the future tense we have noted in other early Christian writers, as it is not found in the Latin version. The use of the indicative, 'you do my remembrance', instead of the imperative, 'do my remembrance' has been thought to be the result of a wrong translation of the Greek verb *poieite* (which can be either indicative or imperative),[54] although again it may be observed that *De sacramentis* 4.26 has a similar phrase, but in the future tense: 'As often as you do this, you will do it in commemoration of me, until I come again.' Finally, it should be noted that, unlike Justin, the account lacks any statement that Jesus then distributed the bread and wine to his disciples.

Taken as a whole, therefore, the impression given is that behind this particular version of the narrative may well lie an independent catechetical formulary of the kind apparently known to both Justin and Irenaeus, but that it has been amplified in the course of its history through the absorption of words and phrases from the New Testament accounts and also by certain variations from those accounts. Although the latter are not encountered within the extant manuscript witnesses to the biblical books, they are for the most part paralleled in one or more other ancient citations and this suggests that they were either current variant readings of the New Testament texts or part of ongoing oral narrative traditions.

The Sacramentary of Sarapion

The eucharistic prayer in this mid-fourth-century compilation of prayers contains what may be the earliest extant example of an attempt to insert the institution narrative into a liturgical text.[55] It is unique in

---

53 *La Tradition apostolique de saint Hippolyte* (Münster, 1963ff.), p. 15, n. 5.
54 Ibid., p. 16, n. 1; G. J. Cuming, *Hippolytus: A Text for Students* (Nottingham, 1976), p. 11; B. S. Easton, *The Apostolic Tradition of Hippolytus* (New York, 1934), p. 73.
55 The other contender for this honour is the eucharistic prayer in the *Apostolic Tradition*. The more polished appearance of the narrative in that prayer could be

that it is not continuous but divided into two discrete parts, separated by other material, including a version of the petitionary prayer from *Didache* 9.4. It is also longer than the other patristic quotations we have observed so far, and lacks any reference to Jesus 'blessing' or 'giving thanks', although mention of the breaking of the bread is included. However, it still seems to be exercising a catechetical function within the prayer, sandwiched as the elements of the narrative are each time between 'because' and 'therefore':

> To you we offered this bread, the likeness of the body of the only-begotten. This bread is the likeness of the holy body, because the Lord Jesus Christ, in the night when he was handed over, took bread and broke (it) and gave (it) to his disciples, saying, 'Take and eat; this is my body which is broken for you for forgiveness of sins.' Therefore we also offered the bread. . . .
>
> And we also offered the cup, the likeness of the blood, because the Lord Jesus Christ, having taken a cup after the supper, said to his disciples, 'Take, drink; this is the new covenant, which is my blood poured out for you for forgiveness of sins.' Therefore we also offered the cup. . . .[56]

The narrative elements appear to be chiefly a combination of components from 1 Corinthians 11 and Matthew's version of the narrative, with words and phrases from the bread unit copied into the cup unit, and vice versa, so as to increase the parallelism of the two. Several scholars have argued that the peculiar form of this whole section of the eucharistic prayer suggests that behind it lay a much older pattern of eucharistic rite altogether.[57] While that hypothesis may have validity, it is hard to be sure whether the particular wording of the narrative units themselves represents the continuation and development of an ancient independent catechetical tradition or whether they have been formed

---

thought to imply that it is later than that in Sarapion, but as developments may not have proceeded at the same pace everywhere, this does not preclude it having attained this form at an earlier date. The Coptic version of the Anaphora of St Basil, which is also often thought to be among the oldest extant eucharistic prayers (see below, p. 151), on the other hand, has an institution narrative that is much more expanded and hence appears later than either of these, but again being composed chiefly of a conflation of 1 Corinthians 11 and Matthew, and also having some similarities with that quoted by Ambrose (*De sacramentis* 4.21–2).

56 For further discussion of the whole prayer, see below, pp. 133–5; for the *Didache*, see Chapter 2.

57 See below, p. 120.

out of the scriptural accounts. However, support seems to be lent to the former view by the existence in other works of parallels to some phrases that do not appear verbatim in any of the New Testament texts. These parallels occur in Cyril of Jerusalem's version of the narrative (see below); in the anonymous treatise *In Sanctum Pascha*, formerly attributed to Hippolytus but probably dating from the second or third century, which quotes the words of Jesus as 'Take, eat; this is my body. Take, drink; this is my blood, the new covenant, poured out for many for forgiveness of sins';[58] in the quotation of Jesus' words by Origen in the third century in works written after he went to Caesarea, 'Take, eat . . . ; Take, drink; this is my blood which is poured out for you for forgiveness of sins. Do this as often as you drink it in my remembrance' (*Comm. in Joh.* 32.24; *Hom. in Jer.* 12); and in the almost identical citation of Jesus' words over the cup by Eusebius of Caesarea in the early fourth century: 'Take, drink; this is my blood which is poured out for you for forgiveness of sins. Do this in my remembrance' (*Demonstratio evangelica* 8.1.78).

Cyril of Jerusalem

In the fourth of the five mystagogical lectures usually attributed to Cyril, bishop of Jerusalem from 350 to 386, the author claims to be quoting St Paul when he says:

> In the night when he was handed over, our Lord Jesus Christ, having taken bread and having given thanks, broke (it) and gave (it) to his disciples, saying: 'Take, eat; this is my body.' And having taken the cup and having given thanks, he said, 'Take, drink; this is my blood.'[59]

However, this is a very adapted version of the Pauline narrative. It adds 'and gave (it) to his disciples' and 'Take, eat' (both found only in Matthew among the canonical accounts, but also included in Sarapion's version, *In Sanctum Pascha*, and Origen), and 'Take, drink' (found in none of the canonical texts, but included in Sarapion's version, *In*

---

58 Text in Pierre Nautin (ed.), *Homélies pascales I* (Paris, 1950), no. 49.

59 *Mystagogical Catechesis* 4.1; Greek text in F. L. Cross (ed.), *St Cyril of Jerusalem's Lectures on the Christian Sacraments* (London, 1951), p. 26. For an account of the debate about authorship, see Kent J. Burreson, 'The Anaphora of the Mystagogical Catecheses of Cyril of Jerusalem', in Paul F. Bradshaw (ed.), *Essays on Early Eastern Eucharistic Prayers* (Collegeville, 1997), pp. 131–51, here at pp. 131–3.

Sanctum Pascha, Origen and Eusebius' *Demonstratio evangelica*). It omits 'which is for you' from the words over the bread and the command to repeat the action from both the words over the bread and those over the cup, and it abbreviates 'This cup is the new covenant in my blood' to 'This is my blood', a tendency going back to Justin Martyr. In spite of Cyril's claim to be quoting 1 Corinthians, therefore, there appear to be signs of some influence from elsewhere. That similar expressions also occur in the Sacramentary of Sarapion, *In Sanctum Pascha*, Origen and Eusebius suggests that all are to some extent drawing on a narrative tradition independent of the New Testament texts. Because the author mentions the narrative in this fourth lecture, where he is explaining the change in the eucharistic elements, rather than in the fifth lecture, where he traces the sequence of the eucharistic rite for his audience, a number of scholars have concluded that the Jerusalem rite did not as yet include the narrative as part of the eucharistic prayer, and this reinforces my contention that the narrative was still viewed as a catechetical text.[60]

---

60 For the arguments concerning the institution narrative and the Jerusalem eucharistic prayer, see Burreson, 'The Anaphora of the Mystagogical Catecheses of Cyril of Jerusalem', pp. 145–8.

Chapter 2

The *Didache*

9.1 *Concerning the thanksgiving, give thanks thus:*
2 *First, concerning the cup:*
We give thanks to you, our Father, for the holy vine of David your child, which you have made known to us through Jesus your child; glory to you for evermore.
3 *Concerning the broken bread:*[1]
We give thanks to you, our Father, for the life and knowledge which you have made known to us through Jesus your child; glory to you for evermore.
4 As this broken bread was scattered upon the mountains and having been gathered together became one, so may your church be gathered together from the ends of the earth into your kingdom; for yours is the glory and the power through Jesus Christ for evermore.
5 *Let no one eat or drink of your eucharist but those who have been baptized in the name of the Lord. For concerning this also the Lord has said, 'Do not give what is holy to the dogs.'*
10.1 *After you have had your fill, give thanks thus:*
2 We give thanks to you, holy Father, for your holy name which you have enshrined in our hearts, and for the knowledge and faith and immortality which you have made known to us through Jesus your child; glory to you for evermore.
3 You, Almighty Master, created all things for the sake of your name and gave food and drink to humans for enjoyment, that they

---

1 The Greek word *klasma* translated as 'broken bread' here and in 9.4 really means a broken piece or fragment of bread, and so seems a slightly odd choice when presumably the bread had not yet been broken. Is it meant proleptically, or is it, as some scholars have proposed, a secondary textual change from *artos*, the normal word for bread? See Arthur Vööbus, *Liturgical Traditions in the Didache* (Stockholm, 1968), pp. 35–9 and 137–57.

might give thanks to you; but to us you have granted spiritual food and drink and eternal life through Jesus your child.

4 Above all we give thanks to you because you are mighty; glory to you for evermore. Amen.

5 Remember, Lord, your church, to deliver it from all evil and to perfect it in your love, and gather it together from the four winds, having been sanctified, into your kingdom which you have prepared for it; for yours is the power and the glory for evermore. Amen.

6 May grace come, and this world pass away. Amen.
Hosanna to the God of David.
If anyone is holy, let him come; if anyone is not, let him repent.
Marana tha. Amen.

7 *But allow the prophets to give thanks as they wish.*

14.1 *Having assembled together on the Lord's day of the Lord, break bread and give thanks, having first confessed your faults, so that your sacrifice may be pure.*

2 *Let no one having a dispute with his neighbour assemble with you until they are reconciled, that your sacrifice may not be defiled.*

3 *For this is what was spoken by the Lord, 'In every place and time offer me a pure sacrifice; for I am a great king, says the Lord, and my name is wonderful among the nations.*[2]

The publication in 1883 of this ancient church order, which has since been variously dated between the middle of the first century and the middle of the second,[3] seemed to present something of a challenge to the view that all eucharistic practice was derived from the actions of Jesus at the Last Supper and recalled that event. Although the meal in chapters 9–10 is designated by the Greek word, *eucharistia*, translated above as 'thanksgiving' in 9.1 and as 'eucharist' in 9.5, scholars have been divided over whether its unusual liturgical provisions are meant to be a Eucharist or not. Clearly if they are, the Eucharist is of a very different kind from those which later became standard. Precisely because of this (and, for some, in particular because the text does not include the

---

2 For the Greek text, see Willy Rordorf and André Tuilier, *La doctrine des douze apôtres* (Paris, 1978, 2nd edn 1998).
3 For the nature of church orders in general, and the questions of date and provenance associated with this particular one, see Paul F. Bradshaw, *The Search for the Origins of Christian Worship*, chapter 4; and for a more detailed study of its contents, see Kurt Niederwimmer, *The Didache: A Commentary* (Minneapolis, 1998).

supposedly consecratory institution narrative), scholars have had to seek ways to account for it. There have been four principal explanations:

I. That it is only ancillary to the Eucharist proper

The earliest solution proposed to the problem, and one which at first became very popular, was put forward by Theodor Zahn, who argued that *Didache* 10 constituted a prayer of preparation for the reception of the eucharistic elements following the meal in *Didache* 9.[4] While Eduard von der Goltz[5] and Theodor Schermann[6] thought that the bread and wine would have been consecrated at a prior celebration of the Eucharist, others regarded *Didache* 10.6 as constituting the point of transition to a full eucharistic celebration following the meal.[7] This theory was later upheld by Willy Rordorf, who even asserted that it was 'the most common view today',[8] and it has also been championed by Kurt Niederwimmer in his recent commentary on the church order.[9] What it fails to explain, however, is why the author of the *Didache* should provide such detailed instructions and liturgical texts for this purely ancillary rite and yet pass over the Eucharist proper with hardly a word. It is not satisfactory to say, as Rudolf Bultmann did, that 'it does not need to be set down because it was familiar to all',[10] as this would also have been true of the baptismal rite and other liturgical practices that are set down in the *Didache*. Nor is it any more convincing to retreat to that hiding place often resorted to by scholars of early Christianity when texts fail to state what one wants – the alleged *disciplina arcani*, the claim that some things are not mentioned in ancient sources because Christians deliberately maintained a rule of silence over their most sacred rites. There are certainly signs of some reserve in communicating the deep truths of the gospel to outsiders in third-century

---

4 *Forschungen zur Geschichte des neutestamentlichen Kanons und der altchristlichen Literatur* III (Erlangen, 1884), pp. 293–8.

5 *Tischgebete und Abendmahlsgebete in der altchristlichen und der griechischen Kirche* (Leipzig, 1905).

6 *Die allgemeine Kirchenordnung, frühchristliche Liturgien und kirchliche Überlieferung* (Paderborn, 1915 = New York, 1968) II, pp. 282ff.

7 For examples, see Jeremias, *The Eucharistic Words of Jesus*, p. 118, n. 3.

8 'The Didache', in *The Eucharist of the Early Christians* (New York, 1978), pp. 1–23. He first put forward this view in 'Les prières eucharistiques de la Didachè' in *Eucharisties d'Orient et d'Occident* (Paris, 1970) I, pp. 65–82. See also idem, 'Die Mahlgebete in *Didache* Kap. 9–10. Ein neuer *status quaestionis*', *Vigiliae Christianae* 51 (1997), pp. 229–46.

9 *The Didache*, pp.142–3.

10 *Theology of the New Testament* I, p. 151.

sources,[11] which might go back to even earlier times; but there is no indication that this applied to the details of liturgical rites prior to the deliberate adoption of a cloak of secrecy in that regard in the fourth century, and the openness of Justin Martyr's description of the Eucharist for pagan readers in the second century[12] would seem to give the lie to that idea.

2. That it is a quite different kind of Eucharist

Another way of accommodating the material in the *Didache* was to postulate the existence of two sorts of Eucharist in the primitive Christian community. Thus Paul Drews proposed that there had originally been a 'private' celebration – a daily religious meal which might be presided over by any member of the community, reflected in *Didache* 9—10 – alongside which there developed before the end of the first century a more official form of the celebration of the Eucharist, held only on Sundays and presided over by a bishop, which was referred to in *Didache* 14.[13] His interpretation was followed by Maurice Goguel and Rudolf Knopf.[14] In his monumental and highly influential work, *Messe und Herrenmahl*,[15] Hans Lietzmann later developed a slightly different theory originally advanced by Friedrich Spitta at the end of the nineteenth century,[16] that there were from the first two quite different types of eucharistic liturgy in the Church. One was the joyful fellowship meal of the early Jewish-Christian communities, the 'breaking of bread' as in Acts 2.42; the other arose within the Pauline churches and was dominated by the theme of the memorial of the death of Christ. According to Lietzmann, the former type was a continuation of the meals shared by the disciples with Jesus during his earthly ministry and was not related to the Last Supper; it had no narrative of institution, did not involve the use of wine and had a strong eschatological dimension, being the anticipation of the messianic banquet. The second type arose from Paul's belief that Jesus intended the Last Supper to be repeated as a liturgical rite ('Do this in remembrance of me' – found only in 1 Corinthians 11.24, 25 and Luke 22.19); it was characterized by Hellenistic sacrificial

---

11 See Paul F. Bradshaw, 'The Gospel and the Catechumenate in the Third Century', *JTS* 50 (1999), pp. 143–52.

12 See below, pp. 61 ff.

13 'Untersuchungen zur Didache', *ZNW* 5 (1904), pp. 53–79, here at pp. 74–9.

14 Maurice Goguel, *L'Eucharistie des origines à Justin Martyr* (Paris, 1910); Rudolf Knopf, *Die Lehre der zwölf Apostel* (Tübingen, 1920).

15 Bonn, 1926; ET = *Mass and Lord's Supper* (Leiden, 1953–78).

16 *Zur Geschichte und Literatur des Urchristentums* (Göttingen, 1893) I, pp. 207–337.

concepts and eventually supplanted the former type everywhere. In spite of its inclusion of a cup, Leitzmann regarded the meal in *Didache* 9—10 as a development of the first type.[17]

Several other scholars adopted variations of this thesis. Ernst Lohmeyer differentiated between a Galilean tradition of bread-breaking stemming from the meals of Jesus with the disciples and a Jerusalem tradition descended from the Last Supper which evolved into the Pauline memorial rite.[18] Oscar Cullmann defended Lietzmann's original hypothesis, but with the qualification that the common origin of both types was to be sought in the historical Last Supper, 'even if only indirectly in the case of the first type'; the direct origin he attributed to the post-resurrection meal appearances of Jesus.[19] While earlier scholars from Spitta onwards[20] had seen a possible connection between the Eucharist and these Christophanies, they had usually viewed the eucharistic experiences of the early Christians as having been responsible for the emergence of the stories, or at least as having influenced their form. Hence Cullmann appears to have been the first to explore the opposite idea, that the resurrection events themselves gave rise to the eucharistic practice, an approach that was subsequently followed by some others, including Willy Rordorf,[21] but has also met with criticism.[22]

The majority of scholars, however, rejected Lietzmann's theory of a dual origin of the Eucharist as being based on extremely tenuous evidence and as making the improbable assumption of a radical dichotomy between the thinking and practice of the primitive Jerusalem church and the Pauline communities, and thus as not providing a plausible context in which to understand the rite in *Didache* 9—10.

---

17 *Mass and Lord's Supper*, pp. 188–94.

18 'Vom urchristlichen Abendmahl', *Theologische Rundschau* 9 (1937), pp. 168–227, 273–312; 10 (1938), pp. 81–99; 'Das Abendmahl in der Urgemeinde', *JBL* 56 (1937), pp. 217–52.

19 'La signification de la Sainte-Cène dans le christianisme primitif', *Revue d'histoire et de philosophie religieuses* 16 (1936), pp. 1–22; ET = 'The Meaning of the Lord's Supper in Primitive Christianity', in O. Cullmann and J. Leenhardt, *Essays on the Lord's Supper* (London/Richmond, VA, 1958), pp. 5–23; see also his *Early Christian Worship* (London/Philadelphia, 1953), p. 17, n. 1.

20 *Zur Geschichte und Litteratur des Urchristentums* I, pp. 292f.

21 *Sunday* (London/Philadelphia 1968), pp. 215–37.

22 See Hartmut Gese, 'The Origin of the Lord's Supper', in idem, *Essays on Biblical Theology* (Minneapolis, 1981), pp. 117–40, here at p. 128; Léon-Dufour, *Sharing the Eucharistic Bread*, pp. 39–40.

3. That it is an agape and not a Eucharist

While some New Testament scholars may have been open to the possibility of two different types of Eucharist in primitive Christianity,
liturgical scholars generally have not.[23] Louis Duchesne was willing to
admit that the rite described was a Eucharist, but he still dismissed it as
'an anomaly; it might furnish some of the features which we meet with
in later compositions, but it is on the whole outside the general line of
development both in respect of its ritual and style'.[24] Josef Jungmann,
on the other hand, simply stated that it was 'hardly likely' that the meal
included 'the sacramental Eucharist'.[25] A more common response was to
regard chapters 9—10 as referring to an *agape* rather than a Eucharist as
such. This was the position taken, for example, by Ferdinand Kattenbusch, R. H. Connolly, F. E. Vokes, and Gregory Dix.[26] However, not
only is this theory open to the same objections as the first one that I
examined – why would the author give detailed instructions for this
meal and not the Eucharist? – but, as McGowan has pointed out, the
whole concept of the *agape* is a very dubious one.[27] It has served as a
useful vague category in which to dump any evidence for meals that
scholars did not want to treat as eucharistic, regardless of whether the
text itself described the meal as an *agape* or by some other title, as here.
What it is particularly vital to note is that there is no evidence at all,
except perhaps in the case of Tertullian,[28] for early Christian communities that practised both a Eucharist and at the same time something else
called an *agape*, but rather that where the latter word is used for a meal,
it seems to be the name of the only form of Christian ritual meal existing
in that community, the equivalent of what other Christian groups might

---

23 A recent exception, however, is Gerard Rouwhorst, 'La célébration de
l'Eucharistie dans l'Église primitive', *Questions liturgiques* 74 (1993), pp. 89–112,
who put forward the idea that there was an annual type, celebrated at
Passover/Easter, which explicitly commemorated the death of Christ and included
an institution narrative, and a weekly type, a Christianized Sabbath meal celebrated
on Sundays and not directly influenced by the Last Supper tradition.
24 *Christian Worship: Its Origins and Evolution* (London, 1903ff.), pp. 52, 53–4.
25 *The Mass of the Roman Rite* (New York, 1951) I, p. 12.
26 F. Kattenbusch, 'Messe', in *Realencyclopädie für protestantische Theologie und
Kirche* 12 (Leipzig, 1903), pp. 671ff.; R. H. Connolly, 'Agape and Eucharist in the
Didache', *Downside Review* 55 (1937), pp. 477–89; F. E. Vokes, *The Riddle of the
Didache* (London/New York, 1938), pp. 197–207; Dix, *The Shape of the Liturgy*,
pp. 48, n. 2, and 90ff.
27 See Andrew B. McGowan, 'Naming the Feast: *Agape* and the Diversity of Early
Christian Meals', *SP* 30 (1997), pp. 314–18.
28 See below, pp. 97ff.

call 'the Eucharist' or 'the Lord's Supper'. So, for example, Ignatius of Antioch appears to regard the words 'Eucharist' and *'agape'* as synonyms when he writes: 'Let that be considered a proper Eucharist, which is (administered) either by the bishop, or one to whom he has entrusted (it). . . . It is not permitted without the bishop either to baptize or to hold an *agape . . .'* (*Smyrn.* 8).

4. That it is an early form of Eucharist

Some scholars were prepared to see chapters 9—10 as a primitive form of the Eucharist, even though it did not reflect the Last Supper traditions and differed from later eucharistic rites. Adolf von Harnack appears to have been the first exponent of this position,[29] and among those who took it up later was Arthur Vööbus.[30] Erik Peterson, subsequently followed by Johannes Betz and Edward Kilmartin, put forward a variant suggestion: that while the prayer texts had originally been intended for a Eucharist, the redactor of the church order had later turned them into *agape* prayers.[31] John Riggs built upon this idea and proposed a more extensive process of development of the texts with several clearly defined stages, in which the core of the prayer in chapter 10 was seen as older than the material in chapter 9.[32] Although his hypothesis is not completely implausible, it does presuppose heavy literary activity in the revision of texts at a period when oral transmission is thought to have been the norm.

While the other explanations I have considered may still command support from some New Testament and patristic scholars, the majority of liturgical scholars in the last thirty years have come round to the view that the rite in *Didache* 9—10 is itself a form of the Eucharist, though without committing themselves to Lietzmann's dual-origin hypothesis, and have modified their own theories about early eucharistic development accordingly. Louis Bouyer appears to have been the first leading

---

29 *Die Lehre der zwölf Apostel nebst Untersuchungen zur ältesten Geschichte der Kirchenverfassung und des Kirchenrechts* (Leipzig, 1884 = Berlin, 1991), pp. 28–36.
30 *Liturgical Traditions in the Didache*, pp. 63–74.
31 Erik Peterson, *Frühkirche, Judentum und Gnosis: Studien und Untersuchungen* (Rome, 1959), pp. 168–71; Johannes Betz, 'Die Eucharistie in der Didache', *Archiv für Liturgiewissenschaft* 11 (1969), pp. 10–39; ET = 'The Eucharist in the Didache' in Jonathan A. Draper (ed.), *The Didache in Modern Research* (Leiden, 1996), pp. 244–75; Edward J. Kilmartin, 'The Eucharistic Prayer: Content and Function of Some Early Eucharistic Prayers', in Richard J. Clifford and George W. McCrae (eds), *The Word in the World* (Cambridge, MA, 1973), pp. 117–34, here at p. 126.
32 John W. Riggs, 'From Gracious Table to Sacramental Elements: The Tradition-History of Didache 9 and 10', *The Second Century* 4 (1984), pp. 83–101.

scholar to break ranks with Dixian orthodoxy on this point, and those who have followed him include Louis Ligier, Thomas Talley, and Enrico Mazza.[33]

Yet this position too is not without its difficulties. There is the need to explain why the compiler of the *Didache* should apparently deal with the Eucharist twice, in chapters 9—10 and again in chapter 14. The usual response is to claim that chapter 14 is an addition to the text by a later redactor and/or that its focus is not on giving directions for the Eucharist as such but on the need for confession and reconciliation before worship.[34] There is also the problem of 10.6, which has seemed at least to some to make more sense as a transition to a eucharistic celebration that follows rather than as the conclusion of the rite. Furthermore, because these scholars wish to adhere to the notion of a single line of development from the Last Supper to the classical eucharistic prayers of later centuries, they are forced to suggest that the prayers in chapters 9—10 are extremely ancient, much older than the church order itself or even the directions that surround them, both to account for their strongly Jewish character and the absence of any reference in them to the death of Christ and also to allow for a sufficient period of time afterwards for their mutation into the kind of prayers it is thought were already in use from at least the middle of the second century onwards. Thus, Mazza claims that the prayer texts must antedate both the composition of 1 Corinthians and also the Council of Jerusalem (48 or 49 CE), because he believes Paul knew the *Didache* prayers and because their primitive Christology would have been unthinkable after the Council.[35]

But such an early dating brings its own difficulties. Although the prayers are very Jewish in character, they also show significant departures from what have been commonly believed to have been the standard Jewish forms of meal blessings already in use. Would early Christians have made such major changes so soon? And why would they have wanted to write them down in any case, since Jewish prayers do not

---

33 Louis Bouyer, *Eucharist* (Notre Dame, 1968), pp. 115–19; Louis Ligier, 'The Origins of the Eucharistic Prayer', pp. 177–8; Thomas J. Talley, 'The Eucharistic Prayer of the Ancient Church according to Recent Research: Results and Reflections', *SL* 11 (1976), pp. 138–58, here at pp. 146–50; idem, 'The Eucharistic Prayer: Tradition and Development', in Kenneth W. Stevenson (ed.), *Liturgy Reshaped* (London 1982), pp. 48–64, here at p. 52; Mazza, *The Origins of the Eucharistic Prayer*, pp. 12–41.

34 See further below, p. 39.

35 *The Origins of the Eucharistic Prayer*, pp. 36, 40 and 90–7. For his claim that Paul knew the prayers, see below, p. 46.

seem to have been committed to writing at this period, and Christian praying otherwise seems to have continued to be extemporized or transmitted orally for a very long time afterwards. In addition, the seemingly unusual 'reverse' sequence from that of the Last Supper, with cup first and then bread, is usually passed over in silence by scholars who support the position that this is a Eucharist, but that might also seem to challenge the idea of a direct line of continuity.

An alternative paradigm

Some – although certainly not all – the difficulties associated with the text could be solved by the adoption of a different paradigm for the evolution of eucharistic rites from that of a single line of development. If the meal in the *Didache* were thought of as simply one of a number of different patterns that existed side-by-side in early Christianity, each being the practice belonging to a particular community or group of communities, then there would be no pressure to slot it into an especially early time-frame. Thus, this apparently 'primitive' practice could well have continued to flourish at a somewhat later date among certain Christians, unaffected by the Council of Jerusalem, even though other Christian groups might already have moved on and were perhaps incorporating a stronger passion motif in their eucharistic praying, had abandoned the custom of a full meal, or had appended their ritual to a substantial ministry of the word. As we shall see in the next chapter, there does exist other evidence that would lend some support to this notion of several parallel forms of Christian ritual meals that only gradually coalesced into the pattern that we recognize as the 'normal' Eucharist. But before we go on to examine this testimony, let us take a closer look at the material in the *Didache*.

The Jewish connection

Quite soon after the discovery of the *Didache* it was recognized that the prayers in chapters 9—10 have a strongly Jewish appearance, and they were thought to resemble what were believed to have been the forms of Jewish table prayers in the first century.[36] Indeed, some commentators

---

36 See, for example, Gottlieb Klein, 'Die Gebete in der Didache', *ZNW* 9 (1908), pp. 132–46; Louis Finkelstein, 'The Birkat Ha-Mazon', *Jewish Quarterly Review* 19 (1928/9), pp. 211–62; R. D. Middleton, 'The Eucharistic Prayers of the Didache', *JTS* 36 (1935), pp. 259–67; Martin Dibelius, 'Die Mahl-Gebete der Didache', *ZNW* 37 (1938), pp. 32–41.

were inclined to make the surprising claim that no more than a few words and phrases had been changed from the Jewish texts on which they were modelled.[37] Attention focused primarily on chapter 10 as resembling what became the standard Jewish grace after meals, the *Birkat ha-mazon*. Louis Finkelstein's study of the earliest extant texts (ninth and tenth century) of this Jewish prayer suggested that something like the following came closest to its early Palestinian version:

> Blessed are you, Lord our God, ruler of the universe, who feed the whole world with goodness, with grace, and with mercy.
> Blessed are you, Lord, who feed all.
>
> We give thanks to you, Lord our God, that you have caused us to inherit a good and pleasant land, the covenant, the Law, life and food.
> For all these things we give thanks to you and praise your name for ever and ever.
> Blessed are you, Lord, for the land and for the food.
>
> Have mercy, Lord our God, on your people Israel, on your city Jerusalem, on your Temple and your dwelling-place and on Zion your resting-place, and on the great and holy sanctuary over which your name was invoked; and the kingdom of the dynasty of David may you restore to its place in our days, and build Jerusalem soon.
> Blessed are you, Lord, who build Jerusalem.

Finkelstein's conclusion after comparing *Didache* 10 with its apparent Jewish counterpart – that the first and second of the three units of the Jewish prayer had been inverted in the Christian version – has generally been followed by other scholars, although Ligier preferred to speak of the first unit being integrated into the second and absorbed by it, so that the theme of creation was subordinated,[38] and Mazza argued that the *Didache* had instead eliminated the first unit altogether and substituted a quite different beginning.[39] Yet the truth is that the parallels exist only in the very broadest of terms, and in any case are of very dubious value. In particular, in their desire to demonstrate similarities, scholars tended

---

37 For example, Bouyer, *Eucharist*, p. 115.
38 'The Origins of the Eucharistic Prayer', p. 177.
39 *The Origins of the Eucharistic Prayer*, pp. 18ff. See also H. van der Sandt and E. Flusser, *The Didache: Its Jewish Sources and its place in Early Judaism and Christianity* (Assen/Minneapolis, 2002), pp. 310–29.

to ignore the structural differences between prayers that begin 'Blessed are you . . .' and those that begin 'We give thanks to you . . .', generally treating them merely as variant translations of the same Hebrew participle, *baruk*, 'blessed'. Even as recent a commentator as Niederwimmer can still confidently assert that the Greek verbs *eucharistein* ('to give thanks') and *eulogein* ('to bless') 'are used unsystematically' in the New Testament and that both translate the same Hebrew verb, *barak*.[40]

The comparisons made by scholars also tend to presuppose that Jewish prayers existed, if not as written texts in the first century, at least in a crystallized form that was relatively unchanging, with no more than minor additions and adjustments being made through the centuries. Yet more recent Jewish studies have questioned that assumption for all liturgy and prayers in the early period with which we are concerned, and argued that 'normative' versions established themselves only very slowly in later centuries, with variant traditions existing in abundance prior to that, and the fixing of precise wording being a very late arrival on the scene.[41]

It is true that in the *Book of Jubilees*, usually thought to have been written in the middle of the second century BCE, there is a form of grace put into the mouth of Abraham that displays a somewhat similar tripartite structure to the *Birkat ha-mazon*: a blessing of God for creation and the gift of food; a thanksgiving for the long life granted to Abraham; and a supplication for God's mercy and peace.[42] And the Mishnah too speaks of a grace after meals composed of three blessings (*Ber.* 6.8), but does not indicate their contents, presumably because they were expected already to be familiar to its readers. Nevertheless, we should beware of drawing too straight a line from these sources to the text first known hundreds of years later. What they show is the existence of a tripartite prayer after meals with a defined pattern. They do not suggest that the detailed contents were already fixed nor that it was the only form in use. Indeed, part of the aim of the rabbinic movement that led to the codification in the Mishnah was precisely to try to establish normative practice from among a range of current alternatives, and the very same passage in the Mishnah itself records the existence of one variant, that a single blessing containing the substance of the three could be said. A fragmentary text of what may be a somewhat different meal-prayer has

40 *The Didache*, p. 144, n. 2. See also p. 8 above.
41 See Bradshaw, *The Search for the Origins of Christian Worship*, ch. 2.
42 *Jubilees* 22.6–9; For ET, see James H. Charlesworth (ed.), *Old Testament Pseudepigrapha* II (Garden City, NY, 1985/London, 1986), p. 97.

survived from the synagogue at Dura-Europos,[43] and also another from the Qumran literature,[44] and so it is quite possible that some traditions within early Judaism had forms of grace that diverged more widely still from this pattern.

Unfortunately, no more detailed information about meal-prayers in this period has been preserved. While, for example, both Josephus and the rest of the Qumran literature witness to the fact that the Essenes prayed before and after eating, they do not give any clear indication of the content of the prayers.[45] On the other hand, the *Letter of Aristeas* refers to prayer before eating as a regular Jewish custom, and the only words that it cites are petitionary rather than an act of blessing or thanksgiving.[46] It should also be noted that Philo consistently uses *eucharistein* rather than *eulogein* to refer to prayer at meals, which may possibly be an indication that there were forms of grace in Hellenistic Judaism which began with that verb,[47] as do the texts in *Didache* 9—10. To this may be added the testimony of the Mishnah with regard to the invitation to pray and communal response which were to precede the grace after meals, and which it directed were to vary in form depending on the number of people present (*Ber.* 7.1–3). That such variation in wording could be tolerated when the Mishnah was compiled seems a strong indication that its text had not been definitively established,[48] and this in turn supports the suggestion that there existed even more diverse forms both of the bidding and of the grace itself which lay beyond the limits that the rabbinic tradition was prepared to recognize.

All this points to the conclusion that the prayers in *Didache* 9—10 should not be viewed as conscious reworkings of existing standardized forms of meal-prayers within contemporary Judaism, with their departures from the norm needing to be explained, but rather as a development out of a variety of forms of such Jewish prayers still in use at the time. We may expect to see some similarities in structure and general themes and other points of contact with the few texts that have survived in the Jewish tradition, but we should not expect to find close parallels. There is a Jewish connection, but it is not in narrow literary terms.

---

43 See Jacob Neusner, *A History of the Jews in Babylonia* I (Leiden, 1965 = Chico, CA, 1984), p. 161, n. 3.

44 Moshe Weinfeld, 'Grace after meals in Qumran', *JBL* 111 (1992), pp. 427–40.

45 Josephus, *Jewish War* 2.8.5; 1QS6.3–8; 1QSa2.17f.

46 *Letter of Aristeas* 185; ET in Charlesworth (ed.), *Old Testament Pseudepigrapha* II, p. 25.

47 See Laporte, *Eucharistia in Philo*, pp. 53–5.

48 *Pace* Joseph Heinemann, 'Birkath ha-Zimmun and Havurah Meals', *Journal of Jewish Studies* 13 (1962), pp. 23–9.

The prayer texts

The texts in chapter 9 generally tend to be passed over almost without comment, with scholars focusing their attention primarily on the prayer in chapter 10 as offering the most fertile soil in which to find the root of later Christian eucharistic prayers. The standard assumption is that once Eucharist and meal became separated in early Christianity, prayers of the type found in chapter 9 would have disappeared altogether or been relegated to the so-called *agape*, and it was prayers of the type in chapter 10 that evolved into the eucharistic prayer over both bread and cup.[49] Yet, as we shall suggest later,[50] prayers of the type in chapter 9 should not be so quickly dismissed. It may be that they actually played more of a part the development of early eucharistic practice than did the *Birkat ha-mazon* and prayers of the type in chapter 10.

It is interesting to observe that the prayer material in chapter 9 is composed of three units, just as the material in chapter 10 appears to be: a thanksgiving over the cup; a thanksgiving over the bread; and a petition for the Church. Neither of the thanksgivings praises God for the food and drink as such, although the first has an oblique reference in the phrase 'vine of David',[51] and the theme of bread is picked up as a simile in the third, petitionary, unit. They are thus significantly different from what are quoted in the Mishnah as later becoming the standard blessings over wine and bread: 'Blessed are you, Lord our God, ruler of the universe, who create the fruit of the vine'; 'Blessed are you, Lord our God, ruler of the universe, who bring forth bread from the earth' (*Ber.* 6.1). The prayers in *Didache* 9 are essentially thanksgivings for the revelation made known through Jesus – and hence an *anamnesis* of him – together with a petition for its fulfilment in the eschatological ingathering of the Church. The attachment of a petitionary unit has no equivalent in the later Jewish tradition of these short blessings. However, in their desperation to find a Jewish parallel for it, scholars have claimed that it is derived from the tenth of the so-called Eighteen Benedictions, the formulary for daily prayer and not for meals, that

---

49   The need to explain how it could happen that a prayer said originally after a meal could have developed into the eucharistic prayer said before bread and wine were consumed has been one of the reasons that have led some scholars to propose that the Eucharist followed the meal in the *Didache*, as we saw earlier in this chapter.
50   See below, pp. 116ff.
51   Niederwimmer, *The Didache*, pp. 145–7, understands this phrase to mean 'eschatological salvation'; Mazza, *The Origins of the Eucharistic Prayer*, pp. 36–7, follows Rordorf in interpreting it as 'the salvific economy realized in the history of Israel'.

probably also did not begin to assume a fixed form until very much later. In reality, the only slight resemblance is that the Jewish text speaks of gathering the people from the four winds of the earth, which is actually closer to *Didache* 10.5 than to 9.4 and in any case is one of a range of similar stock expressions rather than distinctive of any particular formulary: for example, Isaiah 11.12 refers to an eschatological gathering from the four corners of the earth, Zechariah 2.6 uses the phrase 'the four winds of heaven', and Mark 13.27 speaks of gathering 'from the four winds, from the ends of the earth. . . .' In Christian circles, therefore, the apparently brief Jewish prayers at the beginning of the meal have developed into something rather more substantial, both in length and content.

The threefold structure of the prayer in chapter 10 comprises a thanksgiving for other gifts of God brought through Jesus ('your holy name . . . enshrined in our hearts, and for the knowledge and faith and immortality'); praise for the gift of spiritual food and drink and eternal life (without an introductory thanksgiving); and petition for the protection and gathering of the Church into the kingdom, similar in theme though different in expression to that in 9.4. The concluding acclamations in 10.6 continue the eschatological note already struck in the preceding petitionary unit. However, it is the sentence 'If anyone is holy, let him come; if anyone is not, let him repent' that has caused some consternation among scholars. As I have observed earlier, some have seen no other way of understanding this than as an invitation to communion, and therefore concluded from its position that the Eucharist proper must have followed and not preceded this text. But what would 'come' mean in such a context? In later liturgies it might refer to a procession to receive communion, but it seems anachronistic to read that into the text here. The cup and bread are more likely to have been passed around the assembly. Jean-Paul Audet thought that the participants would have moved into another room at this point for the Eucharist,[52] but there is no evidence to support such a conjecture. Could the statement be understood simply as yet another eschatological ejaculation, inviting the holy to join the community of the redeemed and those who were not to repent?

The rubrics

Although many commentators believe that the directives surrounding the prayer texts belong to a later date than the texts themselves, there

---

52 *La Didachè* (Paris, 1958), p. 415.

seems no compelling reason to adopt that view. According to the paradigm outlined earlier in this chapter, the texts need not have been written down until well into the second half of the first century, a period to which the directives could also belong. Two of them, however, call for particular comment.

Didache 9.5 is the earliest explicit prohibition against the unbaptized sharing in the Christian meal, here being grounded in a saying of Jesus recorded in Matthew 7.6 (though it not necessarily quoted directly from the Gospel, as it is also found in the *Gospel of Thomas*). Although Jesus himself seems to have eaten with sinners, and New Testament Christians increasingly shared table fellowship between Jews and Gentiles, the exclusion of those not yet baptized from sharing in eucharistic communion appears to have quickly become standard practice, and is clearly evidenced in second- and third-century sources.[53]

The final directive in 10.7 is also very interesting. Not only does it reveal that in the community, or communities, to which this document relates prophets might still be active and that they might themselves preside over the eucharistic celebrations, it also implies that other ministers, presumably the bishops and perhaps even the deacons mentioned in other chapters of the *Didache*, would not be expected to extemporize their eucharistic praying but use something along the lines of the forms that are set out here. This is very surprising, since all the other evidence we have for the early centuries of Christianity suggests that bishops enjoyed the same liberty of improvisation as the prophets do here.[54] For that reason, the very existence of these written prayer texts from an early date is also surprising. The fact that we do not possess other similar texts from the first three centuries is not just because they have not survived but because Christians generally do not seem to have written down their prayers but preferred oral transmission and improvisation. Perhaps, therefore, there were special circumstances here that led to this unusual step being taken. We may reasonably conjecture that as the number of prophets and other charismatic leaders declined, it became more and more necessary for individual communities to be led by local Christians, elected from among their fellow-members. Because the *Didache* elsewhere finds it necessary to encourage its readers to esteem these bishops and deacons as much as they respect the prophets and teachers (15.1–2),

---

53 See, for example, Justin Martyr, *I Apol.* 66.1, below, p. 61; also McGowan, 'The Meals of Jesus and the Meals of the Church: Eucharistic Origins and Admission to Communion'.

54 See Allan Bouley, *From Freedom to Formula: The Evolution of the Eucharistic Prayer from Oral Improvisation to Written Texts* (Washington, DC, 1981).

the implication is that they did not easily receive equal approbation. Perhaps one of the reasons for this was their lack of liturgical skill in improvising prayer, and this is what resulted in the compiler of this church order taking the unusual step of providing specimen written texts in order to assist them in their ministry.

Chapter 14

A number of scholars have regarded chapter 14 as a later addition to the text of the *Didache* than chapters 9—10 because it seems to return to the subject of the Eucharist that had already been covered there, even if (as some think) only in oblique fashion.[55] Others have rejected this claim, arguing that this chapter is not really intending to give directions about Sunday worship but is focused instead on the particular issue of the need for confession and reconciliation as a precondition of the purity required in the offering of worship.[56] It contains the earliest unambiguous reference to Sunday as the regular day for the celebration of the Eucharist, but as this confirms apparent allusions to that practice in three New Testament texts, it would not be inconsistent with a first-century date for the chapter. Acts 20.7 speaks of a gathering at Troas to break bread 'on the first day of the week', which sounds as if it may have been a regular practice, but that is not said, and it could simply have been occasioned by the particular circumstances of Paul's impending departure. In 1 Corinthians 16.2 the apostle directs that 'on the first day of every week' the believers are to set aside a contribution 'for the saints'. While there is no explicit indication that this was to happen in conjunction with an assembly for worship, it is difficult to see why otherwise this particular day should be selected. Finally, there is the rather more opaque reference in Revelation 1.10 to being 'in the Spirit on the Lord's day' – the same terminology for the day as it used here in the *Didache*.[57]

However, the chapter still raises at least one other difficulty. The phrase 'break bread and give thanks' is an unusual one. Those who believe that the Eucharist followed the meal in chapters 9—10 have seized on the expression in support of their position: thus Audet would relate 'break bread' to the meal for the satisfaction of hunger and 'give thanks' to the Eucharist proper;[58] Niederwimmer thinks it more

---

55 See, for example, Rordorf and Tuilier, *La doctrine des douze apôtres*, pp. 49, 63 and 93.
56 So, for example, Niederwimmer, *The Didache*, p. 194.
57 For further details, see Rordorf, *Sunday*, pp. 193–215.
58 *La Didachè*, pp. 460–1.

probable that the two expressions are 'a hendiadys, together describing the meal celebration culminating in the Eucharist'.[59] On the other hand, 'the breaking of bread' does occur in the New Testament as an early name for the Eucharist,[60] although not explicitly joined to thanksgiving there. Yet, even if it is held to be simply an expansion of that usage, one might have expected the sequence 'give thanks and break bread' rather than the other way round. It could be suggested that 'give thanks' refers to the action in connection with the cup, which would have some similarity with 1 Corinthians 10.16–17: 'The cup . . . which we bless . . . the bread which we break . . .',[61] but then the order 'bread–cup' would be the reverse of that in chapters 9—10.

The strong emphasis in this chapter on the need for the confession of sins and reconciliation before participating in worship sounds as if it is implying the existence of some sort of formal penitential act for the whole congregation. If so, such a practice is without any extant parallels in early Christian literature. Rites to deal with individual instances of very serious sin do emerge somewhat later in the West, but these are not for more general congregational use. Nevertheless, as a similar admonition also occurs in *Didache* 4.14, where the reader is told to 'confess your faults in the assembly (*en ekklesia*)' and not to 'approach prayer with a bad conscience', something public does seem to be in mind. An equivalent instruction is found in the *Epistle of Barnabas*, where again the reader is commanded to 'reconcile those quarrelling' and 'confess your sins' (19.12). The need for moral behaviour to accompany the offering of worship was, of course, a well-established feature of Old Testament prophetic teaching, and was reinforced in a saying of Jesus recorded in Matthew 5.23–4: 'if you are offering your gift at the altar, and there remember that your brother has something against you, leave your gift there before the altar and go; first be reconciled with your brother, and then come and offer your gift.' Although this saying is not expressly quoted here, it may well have been in the author's mind. Instead, a passage from the prophet Malachi is used to support the injunction.

This may be the earliest text explicitly to describe an act of Christian worship as a sacrifice,[62] and certainly appears to be the first to make use

59 *The Didache*, p. 196.
60 See below, pp. 55ff.
61 On this, see further below, pp. 45ff.
62 R. P. C. Hanson, *Eucharistic Offering in the Early Church* (Nottingham, 1979), p. 5, goes against the general consensus by interpreting 'sacrifice' here as the Christian's self-offering of life rather than an act of worship as such, citing as parallels the application of the word to almsgiving in the *Shepherd of Hermas* (*Sim.* 5.3) and to a broken spirit in *Barn.* 2.4–10.

of the quotation of Malachi 1.11 in relation to it, although both become common features in succeeding centuries.[63] The Septuagint text of Malachi is cited quite loosely here, and treated as a command rather than as a prophecy. The quotation combines elements from verse 11 with elements from verse 14 and omits any reference to incense, no doubt very deliberately because of its association with pagan worship in contemporary culture. A similar combination of Malachi 1.11 and 14 occurs in Clement of Alexandria (*Strom.* 5.14.136), although normal Christian usage was to focus on Malachi 1.11 alone, and as a prophecy fulfilled by Christians. While the later use of the text was generally polemical, here its function is to stress the moral purity required of those who are to offer worship, thus linking it implicitly to the sacrificial offering of the believer's life. For the New Testament conceives of the sacrifice that God requires of Christians in metaphorical terms, as being the offering of the whole of life.[64] Thus, for example, St Paul exhorts his readers 'to present your bodies as a living sacrifice, holy and acceptable to God, which is your spiritual worship' (Romans 12.1) – a radical and paradoxical concept in itself, since sacrifice was then generally understood as involving death and not life, and worship as requiring cultic action rather than being 'spiritual', or to translate the Greek word *logikos* more literally, 'rational, reasonable'. This latter idea was drawn from Greek Stoic and Platonic philosophy and already present in the Hellenistic Judaism of St Paul's day, but in his theology it was combined with the notion that it was their *bodies*, their physical earthly bodies, that God wanted and not just their pure minds and souls, as was the case in Greek thinking.

The Old Testament prophets had been insistent that sacrifices and other cultic acts were worthless unless they were accompanied by righteous living, by virtuous acts and just dealings with others, but the New Testament vision went further: righteous living was no longer just to accompany sacrifice; it was itself the sacrifice that God required. Only in the Letter to the Hebrews among New Testament writings do we encounter the idea that words of worship also might be thought of as part of that sacrifice, alongside deeds of goodness and generosity towards others: 'Through him [i.e. Jesus] then let us continually offer up a sacrifice of praise to God, that is, the fruit of lips that acknowledge his name. Do not neglect to do good and to share what you have, for such sacrifices are pleasing to God' (Hebrews 13.15–16). The phrase

---

63 See below, pp. 78–80.
64 On the metaphorical character of Christian sacrificial language, see Gordon W. Lathrop, *Holy Things: A Liturgical Theology* (Minneapolis, 1993), pp. 139ff.

'fruit of the lips' occurs in Hosea 6.2, and was taken up by the sectarian Jewish community at Qumran, who had separated themselves from the Temple cult on the grounds that it had become corrupt and so were no longer able to offer any real sacrifices in the place and in the manner which they believed that God had prescribed. Hence, they came to regard the offering both of a life of virtue and of words of divine praise, 'the fruit of the lips', as an acceptable temporary substitute for the cultic practice. The difference in the case of the Christians was that this activity was seen not as just a temporary substitute, but as the real thing, which the Old Testament practices had foreshadowed and to which they had dimly pointed.

Chapter 3

Other Early Christian Ritual Meals

The *symposium*

As the result of an influential article by Gordon J. Bahr in 1970,[1] a growing trend can be seen among many subsequent scholars to view both Jewish and early Christian meals within the wider context of banquets in contemporary Graeco-Roman culture, and especially the *symposium*, the traditional formal supper, at which drinking wine did not accompany the meal itself but followed it. Here the guests would recline on couches while several courses were served to them, after which they washed their hands before the drinking began. As each bowl of wine was needed, it was prepared by being diluted with something like two to three times its volume of water and then a libation was offered to a particular deity accompanied by a short prayer. But such events were – at least ideally – not just drinking parties. They were as much occasions for conversation, philosophical speculation and the recitation of poetry or mythical stories, as well as for the fostering of relationships.[2]

However, one may challenge the assumption that the precise format of the *symposium* must have been the sole model on which both Jewish and Christian formal meal practice would have been based. There is at least some evidence to suggest that variations of this pattern also existed in the first century. In the material arising from the sectarian Jewish community at Qumran the communal meal is described as involving blessings over the bread and new wine together at the very beginning

---

1 'The Seder of Passover and the Eucharistic Words', *Novum Testamentum* 12 (1970), pp. 181–202 = Henry A. Fischel (ed.), *Essays in Greco-Roman and Related Talmudic Literature* (New York, 1977), pp. 473–94.

2 For more detail, see Blake Leyerle, 'Meal Customs in the Greco-Roman World', in Bradshaw and Hoffman (eds), *Passover and Easter*, pp. 29–61; Dennis E. Smith, *From Symposium to Eucharist* (Minneapolis, 2003).

(1QS6; 1QSa), and later rabbinic legislation in the Mishnah states that saying a blessing over wine before a meal exempts one from the obligation to say a blessing over wine after the meal (*Ber.* 6.5),[3] again suggesting the possibility that wine might be drunk at the beginning of a Jewish meal, before bread was broken. Furthermore, the Roman Emperor Tiberias (14–37 CE) is reported to have introduced the custom of taking an aperitif of wine mixed with water before the meal at the *symposium*,[4] and wine drunk unmixed during the meal itself is attested even earlier.[5] Thus a Christian meal at which the blessing of wine preceded the breaking of bread would not necessarily have been a complete cultural abnormality.

Nevertheless, if *Didache* 9—10 were the only evidence for Christian ritual meals with the order 'cup–bread', we might reasonably be tempted to dismiss it as a mere aberration from the norm. However, there do exist some other signs that the practice may have been much more widespread. I have already referred to the short text of the Last Supper narrative in Luke as a possible witness to such an arrangement, not a particularly strong witness on its own, but perhaps more credible in the light of other evidence, especially that of Paul's First Letter to the Corinthians and of the *Apostolic Tradition*.

Corinth

In conjunction with his quotation of the Last Supper narrative in 1 Corinthians 11.23–25,[6] Paul refers to the Christian ritual meal at Corinth, to which he gives the name 'The Lord's Supper' – a designation for the event not otherwise found in the New Testament and hardly known in other early Christian literature.[7] What is envisaged here is obviously a substantial meal, and Peter Lampe has drawn attention to a form of the *symposium* in the contemporary culture known as the *eranos*, in which participants brought their own food for consumption.[8] This

---

3 See further Andrew B. McGowan, 'The Inordinate Cup: Issues of Order in Early Eucharistic Drinking', *SP* 35 (2001), pp. 283–91.

4 Pliny the Elder, *Naturalis historia* 14.28.143.

5 Diodorus Siculus, 4.3.

6 For this, see above, p. 4.

7 Among its rare occurrences are *Apostolic Tradition* 27.1 and Tertullian, *Ad uxor.* 2.4.

8 'Das korinthische Herrenmahl im Schnittpunkt hellenistisch-römisher Mahlpraxis und paulinischer Theologia Crucis (1 Kor 11,17–34)', *ZNW* 82 (1990–1), pp. 183–213; also his English article, 'The Eucharist: Identifying with Christ on the Cross', *Interpretation* 48 (1994), pp. 36–49.

offers a convincing explanation as to how it could be that the host did not control the serving of the supper at Corinth but 'each one goes ahead with his own meal' (1 Cor. 11.21) without waiting for everyone to arrive or sharing the food equally – the very abuse that Paul is attacking here – and it is certainly in line with later eucharistic practice when members of the congregation brought the bread and wine for the rite.[9]

Scholars have long disputed whether the Eucharist proper took place before, after or during the meal at Corinth. Some have assumed that the Eucharist would have followed the order of Paul's Last Supper narrative, especially as he specifically records that it was 'after the supper' that Jesus took the cup. This would give the sequence: bread ritual, meal proper, cup ritual. But in that case the poor who arrived late (cf. 1 Cor. 11.21, 33) would have missed the first part of the Eucharist. Lampe attempted to solve this dilemma by positing that the rich who came early to eat understood themselves to have been invited to the 'First Tables' and those who came later only to have been invited to the 'Second Tables' or dessert course – a common custom in the surrounding culture. Other scholars have inferred instead that the Eucharist would have taken place after the meal was over, with the cup ritual following directly upon the bread ritual, in spite of the fact that in Paul's Supper narrative they were separated by the meal.[10] But all this is perhaps to impose a completely false matrix upon the material. As we have suggested earlier,[11] when Paul cites the Last Supper narrative it is not to remind the Corinthians of a ritual sequence that they are neglecting but rather to underscore a meaning of the meal of which they have lost sight. There is no necessary reason to suppose, therefore, that the celebration of the Eucharist at Corinth was influenced by the order of the Last Supper narrative at all. After all, most scholars suppose – rightly or wrongly – that by the time that Luke's Gospel was written, the eucharistic celebrations with which the author was familiar no longer followed that order, even though, like 1 Corinthians, the phrase 'after the supper' is included in the longer text of the narrative.

There is, however, another passage in the letter that may shed some light on the ritual pattern at Corinth. In the context of his discussion about the question about eating meat sacrificed to idols, Paul appeals to the eucharistic experience of the Corinthians and poses the rhetorical question: 'The cup of blessing which we bless, is it not a participation in

---

9 See below, p. 83.
10 See, for example, Jeremias, *The Eucharistic Words of Jesus*, p. 121; Schweizer, *The Lord's Supper according to the New Testament*, p. 5.
11 See above, p. 13.

the blood of Christ? The bread which we break, is it not a participation in the body of Christ? Because there is one bread, we who are many are one body, for we all partake of the one bread' (1 Cor. 10.16–17). Nearly all New Testament commentators have dismissed this apparent inversion from the 'normal' order of 'bread–cup' as simply a rhetorical device that enables Paul then to pick up the theme of bread directly in the following sentence.[12] Yet such judgements have been strongly influenced by the belief that there never was a Eucharist with the order 'cup–bread' and by the assumption that the ritual sequence at Corinth must have followed the pattern of the Last Supper as narrated in 11.23–25. Both of these are questionable premises.

Enrico Mazza, on the other hand, has forcefully argued the case that it is 10.16–17 and not 11.23–25 that represents actual practice at Corinth. He denies that the 'cup–bread' order in chapter 10 is required for the coherence of Paul's argument, and claims that on the contrary the theme of unity that is developed in verses 18–22 arises out of both cup and bread. He sees verse 17 as a digression from this argument, and looks to the structure of *Didache* 9 to explain its inclusion, since that text too has not only a 'cup–bread' sequence but also a third unit that connects the theme of the bread with the theme of unity, as here, even though the *Didache* is concerned with the eschatological unity of the Church and Paul with the unity of the assembly sharing in the eucharistic bread. From this he concludes that both rites shared the same threefold structure: a thanksgiving over the cup, a thanksgiving over the bread, and a prayer for unity linked to the theme of bread.[13] Mazza goes further in his argument and alleges that the rite in *Didache* 9 is older than 1 Corinthians 10 because the theological argument of the latter arises out of the text of the former. 'If the text of the *Didache* has parallels with the Pauline description of the Eucharistic liturgy but not with the theology that Paul constructs on the basis of the liturgical text, it is because the *Didache* was not familiar with Paul. Rather, Paul had knowledge of the *Didache*, or of something very similar to it.'[14] Later, he puts his claim even more strongly: 'we can say that the text of the *Didache* is anterior to the First Letter to the Corinthians.'[15]

The last conclusion seems to be going too far. It appears highly improbable that Christians would be writing down the prayer texts to be

12 See, for example, Hans Conzelmann, *I Corinthians* (Philadelphia, 1975), pp. 171–2; Schweizer, *The Lord's Supper according to the New Testament*, p. 4.
13 *The Origins of the Eucharistic Prayer*, pp. 76–90.
14 Ibid., p. 92.
15 Ibid., p. 97.

used at their eucharistic meals within the first twenty years of the movement's origin, especially when improvisation continued to be the norm for the next few centuries. Rather, as we suggested in the previous chapter, the liturgical provisions of the *Didache* seem to have arisen out of a particular – and somewhat unusual – situation that probably belongs to a period towards the end of the first century or even later, when patterns of ministry were beginning to change.[16] This is not, however, to deny the validity of the broad thrust of Mazza's argument, that the general sort of pattern that we encounter later in *Didache* 9 does lie behind Paul's allusions to the eucharistic practice of the Corinthians in chapter 10.

It might be objected that Paul's eucharistic theology points to a rite that would have been much more developed than that of the *Didache*, containing explicit reference to the death of Christ and perhaps even to the Last Supper itself. But such a conclusion does not necessarily follow. As we shall see in a later chapter, even eucharistic prayers that are likely to have been in use in the middle of the fourth century, when eucharistic theology was certainly much more advanced, are still quite reticent in their articulation of that theology.[17] In any case, the fact that Paul feels compelled to give his readers catechesis about the true meaning of the rite itself implies that its import was not fully manifest in the words that were actually used. Even if Paul had instructed the Corinthian church at the time when he originally founded it that the cup that they drank together was a participation in Christ's blood and the bread that they shared was Christ's body, and that therefore they themselves were to treat one another as members of the same body, that lesson had obviously not been reinforced by the words that they said week by week. The result was that they behaved selfishly when they came together, with some going hungry and others being drunk (11.21), so that Paul could not recognize their gathering as a true Lord's Supper (11.20). The Jewish expression 'the cup of blessing' and the ritual breaking of bread were familiar to them, but not apparently the theological interpretation that Paul thought he had previously communicated to them, and hence his need to remind them of it in chapter 11, when he cites the traditional Last Supper narrative that he had passed on to them.

Even the occurrence of the expressions 'eat' and 'drink' (in that order) in 1 Corinthians 11.26–29 does not prove that the sequence of the Corinthian meal must have been food followed by wine. Paul may have been influenced by the Last Supper narrative here, and in any case it

---

16 See above, pp. 38–9.
17 See below, pp. 147–52.

would be the natural order in which to describe a meal, even if the initial blessings had actually been in the reverse order, just as it would in modern speech even if drinks were served before food was put on the table. We may also note the existence of the same sequence in *Didache* 9.5 ('eat or drink') and 10.3 ('food and drink', twice), even though there the blessings clearly occur in the opposite order.

The *Apostolic Tradition*

Although, as was observed in Chapter 1, the church order known as the *Apostolic Tradition* in its extant state dates from the fourth century or later,[18] parts of it have the appearance of being very much older, perhaps as early as the middle of the second century or even well before that. Among these parts are chapters 25—27, not in their present form but in an older recension. Reconstructing that earlier form, however, presents some difficulty, because chapter 25 is extant only in the late and relatively unreliable Ethiopic version, with obvious signs of editorial expansion here, and in chapter 26 what is usually the most trustworthy of the linguistic versions, the Latin, is missing for the first half, and when it does resume it displays a different grammatical construction from the oriental-language versions, raising suspicions about their reliability at this point.[19] In spite of the uncertainty about details, however, what is clearly in mind here is a communal Christian supper involving both cup and bread.

After extensive instructions about an evening thanksgiving for the gift of light, the text continues as in Table 2. As can be seen, it now states unequivocally that this event is not a Eucharist (25.16), but that remark appears to be a comment added by a later redactor rather than an infallible guide to its original meaning, especially as the eucharistic prayer in chapter 4 of the document has the appearance of a later insertion, before which the sole congregational ritual meal referred to in the whole church order would have been this supper. There are also some apparent contradictions in the details of the meal ritual. In particular, does the community share a common cup over which the bishop has given thanks or does each person individually say the thanksgiving over his/her own cup? How can the catechumens share in the meal, albeit

---

18 See above, p. 19.
19 See Bradshaw, Johnson and Phillips, *The Apostolic Tradition: A Commentary* (Minneapolis, 2002), pp. 141–5 and 156–61. Note that chapter 25 = chapter 29C in that edition.

Table 2: Apostolic Tradition 25 [=29C].15–27.1

	Latin	Sahidic	Arabic	Ethiopic
25.15				And in this way, when the psalm has been completed, he is to give thanks (for) the cup and he is to give some of the crumbs to all the faithful.
25.16				And as those believers who are there are eating the supper, they are to take a little bread from the bishop's hand before they break their own bread, because it is a blessing and not the eucharist like the body of the Lord.
26.1	. . . you who are present, and so feast.	And it is proper for everyone, before they drink, to receive a cup and to give thanks over it, and drink and eat, being purified in this way.	Each one before drinking should take a cup and give thanks over it and drink and eat, being pure.	It is proper that everyone before they taste and drink anything, take the cup and give thanks over it and drink and eat because they are pure.
26.2	But to the catechumens let exorcised bread be given and let them each offer a cup.	But let the catechumens be given exorcised bread and a cup.	Thus the catechumens are given the bread of blessing and a cup.	They are to give the catechumens the bread of blessing and a cup.
27.1	Let a catechumen not sit at the Lord's supper.	Do not let the catechumens sit at the supper of the Lord with the faithful.	The catechumens should not sit at the Lord's banquet with the believers.	And catechumens are not to sit at the table of the Lord with believers.

with exorcised rather than blessed bread, and then be denied participation in 'the Lord's supper'?[20] Or are we actually dealing with more than one layer of material here, which has given rise to these discrepancies? Nevertheless, whatever the answers to those questions, it does look as if the cup is meant to precede the bread. Particularly significant in this regard is the sequence of the words 'drink and eat' (26.1), even though in the case of the catechumens the order seems to be reversed: 'bread . . . cup' (26.2). It is also interesting to observe that the word translated as 'crumbs' in the Ethiopic (25.15) represents the Greek word *klasmata*, the word used in *Didache* 9.3–4, and also that the prohibition against the catechumens sharing in the supper is similarly parallelled in *Didache* 9.5.[21]

The latter part of chapter 28 may also belong to this same stratum of material. If so, it contains directions as to what should happen if the bishop is not present 'at the supper': a presbyter or a deacon, if present, may deputize for the bishop and give 'the blessing' – by which appears to be meant the bread that has been blessed – while the catechumens receive exorcised bread. If there are only laity, the bread cannot be blessed.

Papias

Andrew McGowan has pointed out the existence of one more passage in early Christian literature that suggests knowledge of a 'cup–bread' order. The works of Papias, an early second-century bishop of Hierapolis in Asia Minor, have survived only in fragments, but an eschatological passage from his writings that is quoted by Irenaeus speaks of the days coming when vines will produce grapes in enormous abundance, which when pressed will result in large measures of wine, and when ears of wheat will produce grains in enormous abundance, each resulting in pounds of flour.[22] McGowan tentatively suggests that not only the order here but also the fact that the bunches of grapes are said to call out 'bless the Lord through me', taken in conjunction with the other evidence we

---

20 For ingenious attempts by various scholars to reconcile this seeming discrepancy (the catechumens actually stood rather than sat, they ate at a separate table, or they were dismissed after eating but before the Lord's Supper proper began), see ibid., p. 144.

21 See above, p. 38.

22 For the full translation, see Andrew B. McGowan, '"First regarding the cup . . .".: Papias and the Diversity of Early Eucharistic Practice', *JTS* 46 (1995), pp. 551–5, here at pp. 553–4, translating Irenaeus, *Adv. haer.* 5.33.3–4.

have been considering about the pattern of other early Christian ritual meals, might imply a conscious allusion to contemporary eucharistic practice of this kind.

'Wine-less' Eucharists

So far in this chapter we have been examining the evidence for early eucharistic practice in which the thanksgiving over the cup preceded rather than followed the thanksgiving over bread. But that is not the only variation from the alleged normative pattern of the Eucharist that seems to have existed. As well as differences in order, there were probably also differences in the food and drink themselves. In particular, there is evidence that some Christian communities abstained from wine. In Paul's Letter to the Romans, he repeats the admonition he had already given in 1 Corinthians 8.10–13, that those who eat meat should be careful that their actions do not cause others to stumble, because the meat would have been from an animal offered in sacrifice to a pagan deity, but here he mentions not only eating meat but also drinking wine as possible causes of such stumbling (Rom. 14.13–21). Wine is included because it was socially unthinkable in the ancient world to drink wine without a libation to the gods, at least at a banquet if not more generally. In addition, the counsel in 1 Timothy 5.23 no longer to be a water-drinker but to take some wine 'for the sake of your stomach and your frequent ailments' may appear to be merely medical advice, but behind it seems to lie a tradition of abstinence by some believers.[23] Christian groups, therefore, that avoided eating meat and drinking wine in order to distance themselves from any possible suggestion of collusion with pagan religious practices would have been unlikely to make an exception to their rule when it came to the eucharistic meal.

Liturgical historians anxious to trace a single straight line of normative practice from the Last Supper to the fourth century have often dismissed the evidence for the existence of 'bread-and-water' Eucharists as merely a late aberration by clearly marginal and deviant groups. Thus Dix maintained:

> There is no single scrap of the evidence for 'bread eucharists' or 'bread-and-water eucharists' outside the New Testament which can conceivably be dated earlier than *c.* A.D. 150; *i.e.,* it is all later

---

23 For further exploration of the background of these New Testament passages, see McGowan, *Ascetic Eucharists*, pp. 221–33; and for other possible allusions, ibid., pp. 235–8.

than the rise of that wave of ascetic enthusiasm which culminated in a whole group of similar movements classed together by modern scholars as 'Encratite'; some of these were outside and some remained inside the church. But all alike rejected, amongst other things, the use of wine; and to their fanaticism on the subject we can reasonably attribute the disuse of wine in these cases at the eucharist. . . . It also seems quite unscientific to attribute a weight to the tradition represented by these relatively late documents comparable (let alone superior) to that of the statements of I Cor., Mark and Matt., which are at all events first century evidence.[24]

However, if serious note is taken of the witness of Paul to the existence of what may well have been sizeable numbers of Christians in the New Testament period for whom both eating meat and drinking wine presented grave problems of conscience, then there is every reason to suppose that the later practices acknowledged by Dix do have roots stretching back to the very beginnings of Christianity rather than being a later deviation from a recognized norm, even though those subsequent manifestations occur in places geographically far removed from the regions to which Paul's correspondence directly relates. In any case, it is not always realized how sparse is the positive testimony of the New Testament itself to the use of wine in Christian ritual meals. Not only is there the use of the designation 'the breaking of bread' in the Lukan writings (which we shall consider in more detail below) but both in the New Testament and in many other early Christian writings when ritual drinking is referred to, it is almost always 'the cup' rather than explicitly 'wine' that is mentioned, and that includes the Last Supper narratives themselves. While in the material from the Passover tradition wine is expressly referred to ('I shall not drink of the fruit of the vine . . .': Matt. 26.29; Mark 14.25; Luke 22.18), in the description surrounding the interpretative sayings and in the sayings themselves, the word 'cup' is all that occurs (e.g., 1 Cor. 11.25: 'This cup is the new covenant in my blood'). Of course, in these and other such cases in the New Testament and outside it commentators make the assumption that the contents of the cup would have been wine. Very often this assumption may be correct, and frequently there is an indication from the surrounding text to support it (e.g., the allusion to 'the holy vine of David' in *Didache* 9.2; the reference to some participants becoming drunk in 1 Cor.

---

24 *The Shape of the Liturgy*, p. 61.

11.21), but sometimes there is not,[25] and so the identification of cup with wine cannot automatically be assumed in every instance. It is natural to think that the interpretation of the contents of the cup as Christ's blood would have been more lifelike if it was wine that was there, but it is not impossible that at least in some cases water may have been understood in this way.

It is interesting to observe that even Paul himself in 1 Corinthians 10.4 uses the image of water when looking for an Old Testament typology of the Eucharist. Having spoken of the ancestors as having experienced a type of baptism 'into Moses in the cloud and in the sea', he goes on to add to this a type of the Eucharist: 'and all ate the same spiritual food and all drank the same spiritual drink'.[26] The 'food' does not have to be explained to his readers – it is the manna eaten on the Exodus journey through the wilderness – but apparently the drink does, for he continues: 'for they drank from the spiritual rock which followed them, and the rock was Christ'. Now, according to Exodus 17.6, what came forth from the rock in the wilderness when Moses struck it was water. André Feuillet expressed surprise at this use of the water from the rock in eucharistic symbolism and attempted to find an explanation in the image of the banquet of Wisdom, in which wine and water would be the equivalent of one another.[27] But such a solution is unnecessary. If Paul and his readers had been familiar with Christians who used water instead of wine in their Eucharist, even though their own practice was different, such an image would have been perfectly intelligible, and indeed might even have been current in those circles.

The evidence in second- and third-century sources for Eucharists with water instead of wine is sufficiently extensive that it is not easy to dismiss as merely the practices of a few deviant groups and no part of mainstream Christianity. McGowan has assembled a considerable number of possible indications of a 'bread-and-water' eucharistic tradition.[28] Clearly some of these potential witnesses are stronger than others: a good deal of the information comes from the opponents of groups that rejected wine, and so cannot be assumed always to be accurate in their accusations and will probably have played down the extent of the contrary practice. Yet there is enough to imply that the use

---

25 There is, for example, no indication anywhere in the writings of Ignatius of Antioch as to the contents of the cup.

26 We may note that the expression 'spiritual food and drink' is also used in *Didache* 10.3.

27 *Le Christ sagesse de Dieu* (Paris, 1966), pp. 96–7.

28 *Ascetic Eucharists*, pp. 143ff.

of wine was controversial among Christians in at least some geographical regions, and even the vehemence of the attacks by the 'orthodox' on
these supposed deviants is itself evidence that they were seen as a significant threat. Several early witnesses to the use of wine also polemicize
against the use of water in the cup, which would have been unnecessary
were it merely the practice of a few insignificant groups. Preachers do
not usually waste their breath tilting at non-existent windmills, even if
their portrayal of the opposition is not always precisely on target.

In some cases it is apparently within heretical movements that the
practice is located. Thus Irenaeus speaks of a Jewish-Christian sect called
Ebionites whom he assails for using water and not wine (*Adv. haer.*
5.1.3); and Clement of Alexandria refers to a group known as Encratites
who do the same (*Paed.* 2.2.32; *Strom.* 1.19.96). McGowan also argues
that Marcion appears not to have used wine, since Tertullian attacks him
for his hypocrisy in spurning the creator God while still using the
created elements of water for washing, oil for anointing, milk and honey
as food for the newly baptized, and bread for the Eucharist, and yet he
does not mention wine in this list; and Montanists too may also have
abstained from wine.[29] On the other hand, those using water instead of
wine also included some who did not belong to what were regarded as
heretical movements. We shall consider in the next chapter the possibility that Justin Martyr may have been among them, but the clearest
evidence for an 'orthodox' use of water comes from Cyprian. He admits
that while 'very many bishops . . . keep the pattern of the truth of the
gospel and of the tradition of the Lord', there are 'some, whether by
ignorance or naivety,' who offer water and not wine in their eucharistic
celebrations (*Ep.* 63.1). This is obviously not some recent aberration
from an accepted norm, because he later describes it as 'the custom of
certain persons who have thought in time past (*in praeteritum*) that
water alone should be offered in the cup of the Lord' (ibid. 63.14). He
argues at length that wine mixed with water is what 'the tradition of the
Lord' requires, drawing on biblical testimony from Genesis onwards,
and insisting that references to water in the Scriptures relate to baptism
and not the Eucharist, contrary to what others were apparently saying
(ibid. 63.2–12).

Thus, this wide dispersion of instances of 'bread-and-water'
Eucharists across both 'orthodox' and heretical groups is a strong indicator that it was not the preserve of any particular segment of early
Christianity, but rather the survival of a primitive tradition that had
once rivalled the use of wine, and only became pushed to the fringes

---

29 *Adv. Marc.* 1.14.3; McGowan, *Ascetic Eucharists*, pp. 164–8.

later. It is interesting to note, however, that what its opponents assert is not simply the necessity for the use of wine but of the 'mixed cup', that is, wine mixed with water.[30] Cyprian in particular attaches great importance to the inclusion of both wine and water in the cup, understanding the wine to be the blood of Christ and the water to represent the believers, and hence their mingling together to symbolize the union of Christ with the Church that can never again be separated:

> thus, in consecrating the cup of the Lord, water alone cannot be offered, just as wine alone cannot. For if anyone offer wine only, the blood of Christ is dissociated from us; but if the water be alone, the people are dissociated from Christ. But when both are mingled and are joined with one another by a close union, then a spiritual and heavenly sacrament is completed. (*Ep.* 63.13)

The breaking of bread

There is a recurring controversy between scholars who assert that the phrase 'the breaking of bread' was a standard Jewish expression for having a meal and those who insist that it referred only to the blessing ritual over bread at the beginning and should not be regarded as short-hand for the whole meal. Thus, for example, while Dix claimed that 'the phrase to "break bread" is fairly common in Jewish sources in the general sense of to "have a meal"',[31] Joachim Jeremias stated that it 'never refers to a whole meal but only (a) the action of tearing the bread, and (b) the rite with which the meal opened', and he added in a footnote: 'The constantly repeated assertion that "breaking of bread" is an expression used in Jewish sources meaning "to have a meal" is an error that it seems to be impossible to eradicate.'[32] The focus of this debate has been on the occurrences of this and similar expressions in the Acts of the Apostles. It is included in a summary of the life of the earliest Christian community in Jerusalem in Acts 2.42, which is followed by a further reference in 2.46: 'And day by day, attending the temple together and breaking bread in their homes, they partook of food with glad and generous hearts. . . .' Later in the book Paul is said to have gathered with the Christian community at Troas on the first day of the week 'to break bread' (Acts 20.7, 11). To these instances should be added Luke 24.30 and 35, where Jesus is said to have been known to the two disciples at

---

30 See, for example, Irenaeus, *Adv. haer.* 4.33.2; 5.2.3; 5.36.3.
31 *The Shape of the Liturgy*, p. 63, n. 2.
32 *The Eucharistic Words of Jesus*, p. 120 and n. 1.

Emmaus 'in the breaking of the bread'. Finally, there is the account in Acts 27.33–6, where the ship's company have not eaten for days and Paul takes bread, gives thanks to God, breaks it and eats, thus encouraging the rest to eat, but whether this should be included along with the rest as an indication of a specifically Christian practice has been disputed by some. It should also be noted that the phrase recurs in *Didache* 14.1, but there combined with 'give thanks'.[33]

Does the 'breaking of bread' in the above New Testament occurrences indicate a complete meal or merely the consumption of bread in the celebration of the Eucharist? The judgements made by at least some scholars have been strongly coloured by their preconceptions about the nature of the early Eucharist. For example, Dix was anxious to eliminate the possibility that there had ever been a Eucharist without wine and so favoured the interpretation that it referred to the whole meal, including wine. Hans Conzelmann, too, believed that it meant not just the bread ritual at the beginning but the meal itself, while acknowledging that this was a different usage from that in Judaism.[34] Jeremias, on the other hand, understood the Greek word *koinonia*, 'fellowship', in Acts 2.42 as meaning 'table fellowship' and hence referring to the Christian communal meal, while 'breaking of bread' would designate just the eucharistic action, already separated from the meal.[35] While other scholars have generally not supported Jeremias' particular interpretation of Acts 2.42, a number have shared his conclusion that the 'breaking of bread' referred only to the eucharistic action and not a meal. Thus Léon-Dufour reached the opposite conclusion from Dix, insisting that its very name 'implies that it was looked upon as an action independent of the common meal', because he wanted to envisage an early distinction between sacrament and ordinary meal, but then he was forced to assume that the term had been extended to cover 'the sacramental rite as a whole' and not just the bread ritual because he too could not countenance a Eucharist without wine.[36] Apart from Lietzmann and those who have followed his unsatisfactory hypothesis about two sorts of early Eucharist,[37] Jeremias has been one of the few major scholars happy to accept that there had originally been Eucharists that did not include

---

33 See above, pp. 25 and 39–40.
34 *Acts of the Apostles* (Philadelphia, 1987), p. 23 and n. 3; see also Joseph A. Fitzmyer, *The Acts of the Apostles* (New York, 1998), pp. 270–1.
35 Jeremias, *The Eucharistic Words of Jesus*, pp. 120–1.
36 *Sharing the Eucharistic Bread*, pp. 21–8.
37 See above, p. 27. For a critique of its unsatisfactory character, see McGowan, *Ascetic Eucharists*, pp. 25–7.

wine, for he believed that 'the meals of the Early Church were not originally repetitions of the last meal which Jesus celebrated with his
disciples, but of the daily table fellowship of the disciples with him'
(when wine would not have been drunk), and that 'the Christian communities, whose members were mostly from the poorer strata of society,
did not always have wine available'.[38]

On the other hand, the dichotomy being set up in these scholarly
debates between a complete meal and a brief bread ritual may be quite
false. As Jeremias himself observed, for many people at the time, especially the poor, the chief – or even sole – ingredients of the daily meal
would have been bread with salt and water, a point also emphasized by
McGowan.[39] In such a situation, a Christian meal that consisted principally of bread might well be adequately described by its opening ritual:
in this case the breaking of bread really *was* the meal. Indeed, the use of
this term rather than 'the Lord's Supper', apparently current in Pauline
circles, might be an indicator of a difference in what was eaten: 'supper'
in Greek (*deipnon*) would have implied a meal involving more than just
bread, while 'the breaking of bread' certainly would not. It is reasonable
to conclude, therefore, that the author of Luke-Acts envisaged a Christian community meal in which the principal ritual ingredient was bread.
This event would have been intended both to satisfy hunger and to
remember Jesus, with whom the disciples had regularly shared such
meals in his lifetime. The choice of bread might have been solely for
economic reasons but was very probably also influenced by a desire to
avoid elements associated with sacrifice: meat and wine. Whether this
sharing of bread together was understood as participation in Christ's
body cannot be determined from the limited evidence of the Acts of the
Apostles, though the apparent novelty of the addition made to the
Passover story in Luke's Gospel[40] does tend to suggest that it was not.
On the other hand, there appears to be no justification at all for Lietzmann's assumption that instead such 'bread-only' Eucharists were
occasions particularly suffused with eschatological joy. While they may
possibly have been experienced by the participants as an extension of the
fellowship meals shared with Jesus in his lifetime and perhaps therefore
as occasions for continuing encounter with the Risen Lord and of
longing for his return in glory, an ascetic meal composed of bread alone
would more likely be taken as a sign of mourning in the surrounding

---

38 Jeremias, *The Eucharistic Words of Jesus*, pp. 66 and 115.
39 Ibid., p. 51; McGowan, *Ascetic Eucharists*, pp. 79 and 93.
40 See above, p. 9.

culture, and would have been no more or no less joyful in character than meals that recalled the Last Supper and proclaimed the death of Christ until he came again (1 Cor. 11.26).

Was such a ritual meal the same as the 'wine-less' eucharistic tradition that we were examining earlier in this chapter? Though we cannot be sure, it would appear not, but the difference would seem to lie not in whether water was drunk at both types of meal, as it almost certainly was, but in whether there was a cup ritual to which particular significance was given. In the earlier examples the opponents of the practice implied that the cup of water was being treated with a parallel importance to that which they themselves attached to the mixed cup. However, we need to be aware that this may not necessarily be an accurate depiction, but merely a projection of their own outlook towards the cup on to a very different custom. Yet, if there is any truth to their characterization of the practice, then it was probably quite dissimilar from a meal known as 'the breaking of bread', where the cup apparently had no such prominent role.

Evidence from later times in the various apocryphal *Acts* tends to confirm the continuing existence of such 'bread-only' eucharistic celebrations. This testimony needs to be treated with some care, as the *Acts* constitute a very diverse array of literature from different milieux and with different theologies, but that perhaps makes their shared witness to 'bread-only' or 'bread-and-water' Eucharists more impressive. Furthermore, they are composed of stories about the supposed activities of apostolic figures rather than sober accounts of the actual practices of the Christian groups in which they circulated, but even so, it is reasonable to suppose that their descriptions of ritual meals bear some relation to the real customs of those groups. Thus, in the *Acts of Paul and Thecla* 5, Paul's arrival at the house of Onesiphorus is met with the 'breaking of bread'; in the *Acts of Paul* 7 at the conversion of Artemilla, Paul 'broke bread and brought water'; and in the *Acts of John* 72, John goes with others to the tomb of Drusiana on the third day after death 'so that we might break bread there', and after a prayer of praise over the bread they all share 'the eucharist of the Lord' (86). A similar ritual meal involving bread alone is described in a later chapter (109). The *Acts of Peter* speaks of bread and water, described as 'the eucharist', being brought 'to Paul [sic] for the sacrifice that he might offer prayer and distribute it among them', and elsewhere in connection with a baptism Peter takes bread and gives thanks and prays. Similarly, in the *Acts of Andrew* the apostle 'took bread, broke it with thanksgiving and gave it to all'. But it is in the *Acts of (Judas) Thomas* that references to such ritual meals – to which the name 'eucharist' is given – are most frequent. They take place in connection with baptism, and bread alone is mentioned in four cases (27, 29, 49–51, 133), water in included in one (121), and the contents of a cup are unspecified in another (158).[41]

To complete the picture, although the evidence is more limited, there are also some signs that in certain communities other foodstuffs may have accompanied the bread and water (or wine) at the ritual meals and a thanksgiving said over them. Thus oil along with bread, vegetables, and salt appears in one of the eucharistic meals in the *Acts of Thomas*; and salt also features in the Pseudo-Clementine *Homilies*. Furthermore, milk and honey form part of the baptismal Eucharist in several ancient sources; and oil, cheese and olives are provided with prayers in the *Apostolic Tradition*.[42] Both of these may be the remains of eucharistic traditions that once regularly included a wider range of food, and the existence of later ecclesiastical legislation to control what might be brought to the eucharistic table implies that the custom continued to attract popular support.[43] The presence of fish in the feeding miracles in the Gospels (Mark 6.35–44; 8.1–10; and parallels) and in some of the resurrection appearance stories (Luke 24.41–43; John 21.9–13) has also sometimes been thought to imply that it too was a constituent of ritual meals in some circles.[44] McGowan, however, expresses doubts that this was so, because of the silence on the matter in literary sources outside the Gospels themselves.[45]

Conclusion

In this chapter I have tried to delineate the evidence for three variants from the alleged 'normal' pattern of eucharistic practice in early Christianity that seem to have roots going back into the New Testament period: (a) a thanksgiving over the cup first, followed directly by a thanksgiving over bread, most clearly demonstrated in the *Didache* but with possible parallels in first-century Corinth and in the material in the *Apostolic Tradition*, as well as Papias; (b) celebrations using water instead

---

41 For further details on these and other possible instances in all these sources, see McGowan, *Ascetic Eucharists*, pp. 175–98.

42 Details in ibid., pp. 95–127.

43 See, for example, the Council of Hippo, Canon 23; *Apostolic Constitutions* 8.47.2–4; and McGowan, *Ascetic Eucharists*, p. 89, n. 1.

44 See Cyrille Vogel, 'Le Repas sacré au poisson chez les chrétiens', *RSR* 40 (1966), pp. 1–16, and Richard H. Hiers and Charles A. Kennedy, 'The Bread and Fish Eucharist in the Gospels and Early Christian Art', *Perspectives in Religious Studies* 3 (1976), pp. 20–47.

45 *Ascetic Eucharists*, pp. 127–40.

of wine, apparently arising from the avoidance among first-century Christians of elements linked to sacrifice, but continuing to be evidenced in some both 'orthodox' and 'heretical' circles as late as the third century; and (c) celebrations in which bread was the sole, or at least main, element used, first found in the Lukan writings but also in some later Christian groups. In none of the cases that I have examined are there any explicit signs that the ritual meal was understood as related specifically to the death of Jesus or to the Last Supper tradition or as involving participation in the body of Christ. However, that does not necessarily mean that in some cases the connection might not have been made by those participating in it. We know that Paul understood the Eucharist in that way, even though his Corinthian correspondents apparently did not. Similarly, the rite in the *Didache* may not spell out the connection in its text, but that does not prove that those using it did not make the link for themselves. As I have said earlier, some fourth-century eucharistic texts do not seem to have been much more theologically explicit than the *Didache*, even though the eucharistic theology of the period was considerably more advanced than that.

It rather looks, therefore, as though a number of different combinations might have existed in the first 250 years of Christianity's history and not merely the three patterns I have outlined here. For example, there could have been a 'cup–bread' sequence involving water instead of wine, or a 'bread–cup' sequence with water that related itself to a remembrance of the Last Supper. Thus, there does seem to be some justice in McGowan's comment that while his critics tended to argue that Lietzmann had exaggerated the diversity of early eucharistic practice, he had in fact underestimated it.[46] Far from there being just two primitive forms, there appear to have been several.

---

46 Ibid., p. 27.

Chapter 4

Justin Martyr

Justin Martyr provides two successive accounts of eucharistic practice in his *First Apology,* written at Rome about 150 CE. The first occurs in his description of baptismal procedure and the second is an outline of a normal Sunday gathering:

65.1 After washing the one who has believed and assented, we lead him to those called 'brethren' where they are assembled, to make common prayers fervently for ourselves and for the one who has been illuminated and for all others everywhere, that, having learned the truth, we may be deemed worthy to be found both good citizens through deeds and guardians of the command-ments, so that we may be saved with eternal salvation.

2 Having ended the prayers, we greet one another with a kiss.

3 Then are brought to the president of the brethren bread and a cup of water and of wine-mixed-with-water, and he, having taken, sends up praise and glory to the Father of all through the name of the Son and of the Holy Spirit, and makes thanksgiving at length for (our) having been deemed worthy of these things from him. When he has finished the prayer and the thanksgiving, all the people present assent, saying, 'Amen'.

4 Amen means in the Hebrew tongue 'So be it'.

5 And when the president has given thanks and all the people have assented, those called by us 'deacons' give to each one of those present to share of the bread and wine and water over which thanks have been given, and they take [them] to those not present.

66.1 And this food is called by us 'thanksgiving', of which it is permitted for no one to partake unless he believes our teaching to be true, and has been washed with the washing for forgiveness of sins and regeneration, and so lives as Christ handed down.

2 For not as common bread or common drink do we receive these things; but just as our Saviour Jesus Christ, being incarnate through (the) word of God, took both flesh and blood for our salvation, so too we have been taught that the food over which thanks have been given through (a) word of prayer which is from him,[1] from which our blood and flesh are fed by transformation, is both the flesh and blood of that incarnate Jesus.

3 For the apostles in the memoirs composed by them, which are called gospels, have handed down what was commanded them: that Jesus having taken bread, having given thanks, said, 'Do this in my remembrance; this is my body'; and similarly having taken the cup and having given thanks, said, 'This is my blood'; and gave to them alone.

4 And the evil demons, having imitated this, have handed it down to be done also in the mysteries of Mithras. For as you either know or can learn, bread and a cup of water are used in the rites of initiation with certain formulas.

67.1 And afterwards we continually remind one another of these things. Those who have provide for all those in need; and we are always together with one another.

2 And for all the things with which we are supplied we bless the Maker of all through his Son Jesus Christ and through the Holy Spirit.

3 And on the day called 'of the Sun' an assembly is held in one place of all living in town or country, and the memoirs of the apostles or the writings of the prophets are read for as long as time allows.

4 Then, when the reader has finished, the president in a discourse makes an admonition and exhortation for the imitation of these good things.

5 Then we all stand up together and send up prayers; and as we said before, when we have finished the prayer, bread and wine and water are brought, and the president likewise sends up prayers and thanksgivings according to his ability, and the people assent, saying the Amen; and the distribution and participation by everyone in those things over which thanks have been given takes place; and they are sent to those not present through the deacons.

---

1 For the reading and meaning of this particular phrase, see the discussion below, pp. 92–3.

6 And those who have the means and so desire give what they wish, each according to his own choice; and what is collected is deposited with the president.

7 And he provides for both orphans and widows, and those in need through sickness or through other cause, and those who are in prison, and strangers sojourning, and, in a word, he becomes a protector for all those who are in want.

8 And we all make an assembly together on Sunday, because it is the first day, on which God, having transformed the darkness and matter, made the world; and Jesus Christ our Saviour rose from the dead the same day; for they crucified him the day before Saturday; and the day after Saturday, which is Sunday, appearing to his apostles and disciples, he taught these things which we have also presented to you for consideration.

The conventional view is that we have here the oldest description of the pattern of eucharistic worship (a) after it had become separated from a full meal, when, as a result of this, (b) it was transferred from the evening to the morning, and (c) on a normal (i.e., non-baptismal) Sunday appended to a service of the word that already existed at that hour and was modelled on the Jewish Sabbath day liturgy; and (d) the sevenfold eucharistic action of New Testament times was collapsed into a four-action shape – taking bread and wine together, saying a eucharistic prayer over both, breaking the bread, and distributing the bread and wine to the congregation – that was to become the classic pattern of the Eucharist ever after.

However, the situation might not be quite as straightforward as that. But before examining the evidence in detail, we need to remind ourselves of the nature of this particular text. The *First Apology* was addressed, at least ostensibly, to the emperor Antoninus Pius and obviously intended to explain Christianity to those outside the faith. Thus we may rightly ask whether this has affected the sort of detail that Justin chooses to give, and not give, in his account of the Eucharist, and the manner in which he describes particular practices. Similarly, we might wonder whether he is intending to give a report of the specific form of worship practised in Rome at this time or rather to offer a more generic description of the sort of worship that might be encountered by his readers in various parts of the world. In any case, the idea that there was a single church in Rome at this period seems to be anachronistic: instead, there appears to have been a somewhat loose collection of Christian communities distinguished from one another by significant ethnic – and probably also liturgical –

differences.[2] Since Justin himself was Syrian in origin, and had been baptized at Ephesus, he would have belonged to a community at Rome that was primarily Eastern in membership and would not necessarily have been very familiar with what went on in other Christian assemblies in the city, a conclusion that seems to be confirmed by passages in his *Acts*.[3]

Separation from the meal?

There has been a widely held view among scholars that meal and Eucharist, though still combined, were nevertheless clearly distinguished from one another at a very early point in Christianity's history, with meal following Eucharist or Eucharist following meal.[4] There has been less agreement, however, as to when the two finally parted company. While some have assigned this step to the second century, others have thought that it came about very much earlier. Dix, as we have seen, believed that it happened 'after the writing of I Cor. but before the writing of the first of our gospels'.[5]

Both of the presuppositions that lie behind this conventional picture of the development of the early rite – that Eucharist and meal were distinguishable from one another at a very early date and that the two eventually became separated from each other everywhere – can be questioned. There is no actual evidence at all that Eucharist and meal were ever distinguished in this way in primitive Christianity. On the contrary, it seems to be a pure product of the minds of modern scholars who find it impossible to imagine that early Christians might have viewed the whole meal as sacred – as 'the Eucharist'. Hence they assume that, like later Christians, those early believers would instead have wanted to draw a clear line between 'the sacramental rite' and 'ordinary food'. Similarly, while it is true that in places where the meal had been composed of a variety of foodstuffs, it would eventually have become necessary for

---

2 See A. Hamman, 'Valeur et signification des renseignements liturgiques de Justin', *SP* 13 (1975), pp. 364–74; G. La Piana, 'The Roman Church at the End of the Second Century', *HTR* 18 (1925), pp. 214–77; Peter Lampe, *Die städtrömischen Christen in den ersten beiden Jahrhunderten* (Tübingen, 1987); ET = *From Paul to Valentinus: Christians at Rome in the First Two Centuries* (Minneapolis/London, 2003).

3 *Acts of Justin* 3.3; 4.7-8, in H. Mursillo (ed.), *The Acts of the Christian Martyrs* (Oxford, 1972), pp. 44–5. See McGowan, *Ascetic Eucharists*, pp. 154–5.

4 For example, see above, p. 45, concerning the order of the Eucharist at Corinth, and p. 56 for Léon-Dufour's interpretation of the breaking of bread in Acts.

5 See above, p. 12.

everything except the bread and cup to be eliminated altogether or transferred to a different occasion, there are no real grounds for supposing that this happened at an early date, nor would it have happened at all in those communities where bread, salt and water formed the complete meal. As indicated in the previous chapter,[6] though frugal, this might not have been as unusual to Jews and others in the ancient world as it appears to modern eyes, since for many poorer people in the ancient world, meat was no more than an occasional luxury and in any event for Christians it was tainted by its connection with pagan sacrifice. In such situations, what took place was not so much the separation of meal from Eucharist as simply a reduction in quantity, from substantial portions to no more than token amounts, and it is much more difficult to determine from the limited nature of the evidence just when this might have come about.

A letter to the Emperor Trajan from Pliny the Younger, the Roman governor in Bithynia, has sometimes been cited as evidence that meal and Eucharist had already been separated by the time that it was written (*c.* 112 CE), because Pliny speaks of two distinct regular Christian gatherings on a fixed, though unspecified, day (*stato die*), one 'before daylight' and the other later, presumably in the evening (*Ep.* 10.96). At the morning meeting the local Christians are said to have 'sung a hymn (*carmen*) to Christ as God' and 'bound themselves by an oath (*sacramentum*) not for any crime, but not to commit theft or robbery or adultery . . .', while at the later meeting they took 'food, but of an ordinary and harmless kind' (*cibum promiscuum tamen et innoxium*).[7] Pliny states that they had now given up this latter assembly after his edict forbidding the existence of clubs, and so some modern scholars have seen this as the abandonment of the full meal in favour of the eucharistic celebration on its own, which would then have become attached to the morning meeting instead. However, because the interpretation of Pliny's account is surrounded with so many uncertainties, not least because Pliny himself had no first-hand knowledge of what was being reported to him, other scholars have hesitated to make use of this letter as a trustworthy source for what Christians were actually doing. In particular, the exact nature of the morning meeting, and hence of the

---

6 See above, p. 57.

7 The emphasis put by the Christians on the food being of an ordinary and harmless kind was no doubt intended to counter common accusations from their pagan contemporaries that they indulged in cannibalism and other deviant activities: see Andrew B. McGowan, 'Eating People: Accusations of Cannibalism Against Christians in the Second Century', *JECS* 2 (1994), pp. 413–42.

meaning of the words *carmen* and *sacramentum* here, has been questioned: Was it a baptismal rite or a service of the word, or even a Eucharist already separated from the meal in the evening?[8] A baptism may seem unlikely to have been a regular weekly occurrence, but how could a service of the word be said to include an 'oath', unless the recitation of the Decalogue is what was intended? Or had Pliny misunderstood what *sacramentum* meant here? In any case, his ban on clubs would have applied only in that one province, and so cannot be used to explain changes in the practice of Christians elsewhere. While there might have been similar bans in other provinces, we have no evidence at all for them.

It was more probably the increase in the size of Christian congregations that was generally responsible for the meal eventually being given up or severely curtailed in quantity, as seating and catering for large numbers for a substantial supper then became impossible and local churches outgrew the houses that were first used as their meeting-places. That, at least as far as north Africa was concerned, seems to be the implication of a remark by Cyprian in the third century about the abandonment of the supper in larger congregations.[9] Dining rooms even in substantial private houses would not normally have accommodated more than about a dozen persons, and it is unlikely that Christians would have wanted to rent out the dining spaces attached to pagan temples, which would have been the usual solution adopted by others to the problem of larger parties. On the other hand, if the atrium area of the home was also used for dining, up to forty or fifty people might have been accommodated, but greater numbers than that would have put an end to the older forms of the meal.[10]

The *terminus ad quem* for this development has to be the end of the use of private homes and their replacement by specially adapted buildings that would accommodate larger congregations. Although the Eucharist might have become detached from the meal well before this, it must have done so by the time of this change. Modern architectural historians usually date it as taking place from the middle of the second century onwards, although recognizing that at least some communities may have been able to persist with the former arrangement for a considerable time after this.[11] In fact, the earliest direct literary and

---

8 For the various points of view, see the works cited in David H. Tripp, 'Pliny and the Liturgy: yet again', *SP* 15 (1984), pp. 581–5; and J. C. Salzmann, 'Pliny (*ep.* 10,96) and Christian Liturgy – A Reconsideration', *SP* 20 (1989), pp. 389–95.
9 *Ep.* 63.16.1. See below, p. 109.
10 See Jerome Murphy-O'Connor, *St Paul's Corinth: Texts and Archeology* (Wilmington, DE, 1983), pp. 153–67.
11 See White, *Building God's House*, esp. pp. 119–20.

archaeological evidence for the change only emerges in the third century, and it appears to be Jeremias' assumption that the mid-second-century *Epistula Apostolorum* describes an Easter liturgy in which *agape* and Eucharist had already been separated that has been a major factor in encouraging the idea that the process began at a much earlier date.[12] This apocryphal work is extant only in Coptic and Ethiopic versions of a presumed Greek original. In the Ethiopic Jesus speaks of the apostles celebrating 'my *agape* and my remembrance' and in the Coptic of 'the remembrance that is for me and the *agape*'.[13] However, this is not the only possible, nor necessarily the most natural, interpretation of the text. There is no reason to suppose that '*agape*' and 'remembrance' are two separate events here rather than two ways of speaking about the same thing: the Easter Eucharist/*agape* celebrated in remembrance of Jesus.

Justin's statement that 'an assembly is held in one place of all who live in town or country' (67.3) might be cited in favour of a separation having already taken place, as it could be understood as implying that the congregation must have been of some considerable size. But the phrase translated here as 'in one place' (*epi to auto*), common in classical Greek and the Septuagint, seems to have acquired a quasi-technical sense in early Christian writings as signifying the union of the Christian body rather than necessarily the physical presence of everyone in the same location;[14] and Justin's own response to the question 'Where do you assemble?', when he was being examined by the Roman prefect Rusticus, 'Do you suppose we can all meet in the same place?', appears to confirm that is its meaning here too.[15]

Thus, if the meal had always been one of bread and cup alone in the tradition that Justin is describing and the congregation was still relatively small, then no change might yet have taken place. This could affect our understanding of Justin's statement that the deacons take to those who are absent a portion of what is consumed by those present

---

12 *The Eucharistic Words of Jesus*, p. 116. See White, *Building God's House*, p. 119, n. 62.

13 Ethiopic chapter 15; ET in Wilhelm Schneemelcher (ed.), *New Testament Apocrypha* I (2nd edn, Cambridge, 1991), pp. 249–84, here at p. 258.

14 Acts 1.15; 2.1, 47; 1 Cor. 11.20; 14.23; *1 Clement* 34.7; *Barnabas* 4.10; Ignatius, *Eph.* 5.3; 13.1; *Magn.* 7.1; *Phil.* 10.1. See Bruce Metzger, *A Textual Commentary on the Greek New Testament* (London, 1971), p. 305; Max Wilcox, *The Semiticisms of Acts* (Oxford, 1965), pp. 95–100; Everett Ferguson, 'When You Come Together: *Epi to Auto* in Early Christian Literature', *Restoration Quarterly* 16 (1973), pp. 202–8.

15 *Acts of Justin* 3.1, in Mursillo (ed.), *The Acts of the Christian Martyrs*, pp. 44–5.

(65.5; 67.5) – the earliest reference to a custom that later became standard practice – for this might not have been merely a token amount, but enough to give them a meal of equivalent size to that eaten by the other participants. It was not unusual in Graeco-Roman culture for a wealthy patron sometimes to make donations of food to those who depended on him instead of inviting them to share in a meal at his house,[16] and so Christians might well have done the same for any of their number who could not be present and who might therefore go hungry because their poverty made it difficult for them to afford food. A practice of this kind seems to be referred to in *Apostolic Tradition* 28 and 30, where the two possibilities of a Christian host providing either a meal at his house (with leftovers being sent to others) or instead donations of food and wine to take away are both mentioned.[17] Even if by Justin's day the eucharistic celebration did consist of only token amounts, the origin of the practice of also sharing these with other Christians unable to be present may well have its roots in this charitable tradition. We may note that giving by the wealthy members of the congregation for the needs of the poor is mentioned in conjunction with this ministry in 67.6–7. This practice had already been touched on more briefly in 67.1, and had also been referred to earlier by Paul in 1 Corinthians 16.2. The connection of the Eucharist with giving to those in need continued to be maintained in later Christian tradition, thus reinforcing the intimate relationship that was understood to exist between the shared meal and the mutual love expected of the participants – the failure of which was the very basis of Paul's criticism of the Corinthians (1 Cor. 11).

The hour of celebration?

It is not until the third century that we encounter any indications in literary sources that the Eucharist might have been celebrated in the morning rather than the evening.[18] But was it already a longstanding tradition? As we have seen above, scholars have usually supposed that it was, because they have believed that the separation of Eucharist from meal would have taken place very much earlier and that the alteration in the hour of celebration would have accompanied that change. Justin's

---

16 See the references in Charles A. Bobertz, 'The Role of Patron in the *Cena Dominica* of Hippolytus' *Apostolic Tradition*', *JTS* 44 (1993) 170–84, here at pp. 175–6.
17 See Bradshaw, Johnson and Phillips, *The Apostolic Tradition*, pp. 146–51 and 162–3.
18 See below, pp. 99 and 109.

account does not explicitly indicate any particular time of day, even though liturgical historians have usually assumed that morning was meant, and thus it is at least as compatible with an evening assembly as a morning one.[19] But if it were an evening gathering, which evening would it have been – Saturday evening, which according to the Jewish reckoning of days was regarded the beginning of the first day of the week, or Sunday evening? Against the general consensus of scholars, Willy Rordorf argued at length for the latter as having been the practice from the very beginnings of Christianity, but his thesis has not won general acceptance.[20] It seems more probable that the first Jewish-Christians would have centred their remembrance of Jesus on the traditional festal meal held each week at the conclusion of the Sabbath, understood eventually as being the beginning of the first day of the week, rather than through the creation of a completely new occasion twenty-four hours later.

Yet, would Justin have described Saturday evening to the Emperor as being 'on the day called of the Sun' (67.3), when the Roman reckoning of the day ran from midnight to midnight? This factor might be the one to tip the balance of probability in favour of Justin having in mind a eucharistic celebration that had been transferred from Saturday evening to early on Sunday morning, before the day's work began – that is, unless of course he was simply wanting to distance the Christian observance from the Jewish, and so stated that it took place on Sunday when strictly, in Roman terms, it should have been called Saturday. Others might want to add to this the argument that the service of the word and prayers described by Justin as preceding the eucharistic action is unlikely to have been prefixed to an evening meal, and more likely to have been a pre-existing morning service to which the Eucharist was then attached. This claim, however, requires more detailed consideration, to which we now turn.

Fusion with a synagogue-style liturgy of the word?

That the Christian Eucharist became appended to a service of the word modelled after the Jewish synagogue service has been an unquestioned

---

19 See M. Klinghardt, *Gemeinschaftsmahl und Mahlgemeinschaft. Soziologie und Liturgie frühchristlicher Mahlfeiern* (Tübingen, 1996), pp. 501–2.

20 *Sunday*, esp. pp. 54–153 and 215–73. See the critique of his argument and that of others on the Sabbath/Sunday relationship in the outstanding essay by Gerard Rouwhorst, 'The Reception of the Jewish Sabbath in Early Christianity', in Paul Post et al. (eds), *Christian Feast and Festival* (Leuven, 2001), pp. 223–66.

assumption of liturgical scholarship for more than a century,[21] and until recently it would have been difficult to find any scholar, Jewish or Christian, who would have questioned that there did exist a well-defined Sabbath synagogue liturgy in the first century of the Common Era. However, on the basis of both archaeological and literary evidence, a growing number of scholars now doubt that a Sabbath liturgy in the sense in which it was later understood was a characteristic of the synagogue before the third century.[22] Instead, it seems to have been a lengthy meeting for the primary purpose of reading and studying a portion of the Torah on every Sabbath and festival that was a regular feature of the synagogue from the outset, and may even have constituted *the* fundamental reason for the emergence of that institution. So lengthy might the assembly be that Philo reports that in Alexandria it did not end until the late afternoon (*Apol.* 7.12–13). This practice of study-as-worship might well also have included some actual praying, but probably not the formalized and regulated patterns of prayer that are prefixed to it in the synagogue liturgy of subsequent centuries.[23] There is also evidence for similar gatherings on Mondays and Thursdays, the two regular days of fasting in the week, and Luke 4.16–30 and Acts 13.15 indicate that by the first century the Sabbath assembly already included a further reading from the Prophets (which in the Jewish division of the Scriptures includes the historical books of Joshua, Judges, Samuel and Kings). It is unlikely that any standardized lectionary had by then emerged to govern either the reading from the Torah or that from the Prophets.

It is generally assumed that it would have been a simple and natural step for the earliest Christians then to transfer this Sabbath meeting to Sunday mornings instead, in order to differentiate themselves from other Jews. But this is to imagine that, on the one hand, early Jewish Christians would have wanted to give up the observance of the Sabbath, of which this assembly was a part, and on the other hand Gentile Chris-

---

21 See, for example, Dix, *The Shape of the Liturgy*, pp. 36ff.

22 See, for example, the detailed study by Heather A. McKay, *Sabbath and Synagogue: The Question of Sabbath Worship in Ancient Judaism* (Leiden, 1994); and the briefer survey by Daniel K. Falk, 'Jewish Prayer Literature and the Jerusalem Church in Acts', in Richard Bauckham (ed.), *The Book of Acts in its Palestinian Setting* (Carlisle/Grand Rapids, 1995), pp. 267–301, here at pp. 277–85. McKay has been rightly criticized by Pieter van der Horst, 'Was the synagogue a place of Sabbath worship before 70 C.E.?', in Steven Fine (ed.), *Jews, Christians and Polytheists in the Ancient Synagogue* (London/New York, 1999), pp. 18–43, for defining 'worship' too narrowly and ignoring the probability that study included some prayer.

23 On this, see further Lee Levine, *The Ancient Synagogue* (New Haven, CT, 2000), pp. 151–5.

tians would have been eager to adopt this Jewish assembly, albeit on a different day. Both these suppositions are very dubious. We know, both from the preservation in the Synoptic Gospels of stories of disputes between Jesus and the Pharisees over the keeping of the Sabbath and also from the polemic against the practice in other early literary sources,[24] that some Christians were continuing to observe the Sabbath and that this was a contentious issue. Conversely, there are signs that other Christians may have known a ministry of the word already associated with the eucharistic meal in the first century rather than as a separate institution. Luke tells the story of Paul addressing the community at Troas 'gathered to break bread' on the first day of the week, and prolonging his speech until midnight before they ate (Acts 20.7, 11), and also of the risen Jesus interpreting 'in all the scriptures the things concerning himself' to the disciples on the road to Emmaus prior to his being 'known to them in the breaking of the bread' in the evening (Luke 24.13–35). While other explanations can be – and have been – advanced for these two incidents,[25] it is at least possible that they reflect a regular practice known to the author of prefixing the meal with some sort of teaching/exhortation.[26] Similarly, Paul's sole reference in his letters to the existence of a ministry of the word suggests an assembly of a very different kind from the synagogue study of the Law and the Prophets (1 Cor. 14.26: 'When you come together, each one has a hymn, a teaching, a revelation, a tongue, or an interpretation'), and while there is no explicit indication as to when this might have occurred, it could have come at the end of the eucharistic meal referred to earlier in the letter (1 Cor. 10–11),[27] especially as similar informal activities of this kind are reported at ritual meals both in Jewish practice and also in the later Christian tradition.[28] It is implausible for it to have been at the

---

24 See, for example, *Barn.* 15.8–9, which speaks of keeping 'the eighth day' rather than the Sabbath; and Ignatius, *Magn.* 9.1, which speaks of observing 'the Lord's Day' in place of the Sabbath.

25 See, for example, John E. Alsup, *The Post-Resurrection Appearance Stories of the Gospel Tradition* (London, 1975), pp. 197–9; Conzelmann, *The Acts of the Apostles*, p. 169.

26 See, for example, Léon-Dufour, *Sharing the Eucharistic Bread*, pp. 27–8; Fitzmyer, *The Acts of the Apostles*, pp. 668–9.

27 So, for example, C. K. Barrett, *A Commentary on the First Epistle to the Corinthians* (London, 1968), p. 325; Smith, *From Symposium to Eucharist*, pp. 200ff.

28 See the account by Philo of the Jewish Therapeutae singing together before and after their festal meals (*De vita contemplativa* 80-4); the account by Tertullian of a similar Christian practice after a shared meal (*Apol.* 39; below, p. 99); and *Apostolic Tradition* 28, where the bishop exhorts the community assembled for a meal (Bradshaw, Johnson and Phillips (eds), *The Apostolic Tradition*, pp. 146–51).

beginning of the gathering, before the meal, because then the latecomers (cf. 1 Cor. 11.33) would have missed it.

What seems more probable, therefore, is that predominantly Gentile congregations are less likely to have replicated the Jewish assemblies for study in their patterns of worship but developed different forms of ministry of the word either before or after their Saturday evening eucharistic meal, while conversely congregations with stronger Jewish foundations are more likely to have retained the traditional assembly on the Sabbath itself at first and only very much later, perhaps as Jewish influence slowly waned, to have transferred it to Sunday to accompany the eucharistic rite[29] – or maybe even repeated it on that day while retaining it on the Sabbath. Both developments thus owe their origin to the synagogue, but in the former case the influence is more indirect than direct. This proposal also helps to explain why in some churches, especially those of Syria with their strongly Semitic character, Saturdays continued to be regarded with special honour, as days when fasting was not permitted and on which in the fourth century the Eucharist was regularly celebrated; and why in those same churches the ministry of the word in the Sunday Eucharist came to include Old Testament as well as New Testament readings. By contrast, in other churches without such roots, especially those in the West, Saturdays were not so regarded, fasting was permitted then, and the eucharistic liturgy did not regularly include Old Testament readings.[30]

What still remains something of a mystery, however, is why either of these traditions should eventually have moved the Eucharist from Saturday evening to Sunday morning at all. The disappearance of a full meal does not of itself seem to provide sufficient grounds for changing the time of the gathering, although if some groups within a congregation continued to share suppers together at the original time, a different occasion would then have had to be sought for the Eucharist proper. It is not impossible that a separate service of the word already existed on

---

29 See Harald Riesenfeld, *The Gospel Tradition* (Oxford, 1970), pp. 125–37; Stephen G. Wilson, *Related Strangers. Jews and Christians 70–170 C.E.* (Minneapolis, 1995), p. 233. Alistair Stewart-Sykes, *The Life of Polycarp* (Sydney, Australia, 2002), pp. 66–7, has also put forward the intriguing suggestion that the 'fixed day' in Pliny's letter (see above, p. 65) may not have been Sunday, as has almost universally been presumed, but Saturday, and hence evidence for a pattern of a service of the word in the morning and a gathering for a eucharistic meal in the evening.

30 See Gerard Rouwhorst, 'Continuity and Discontinuity between Jewish and Christian Liturgy', *Bijdragen* 54 (1993), pp. 72–83; idem, 'The Reading of Scripture in Early Christian Liturgy', in Leonard V. Rutgers (ed.), *What Athens has to do with Jerusalem* (Leuven, 2002), pp. 305–31.

Sunday mornings before this and so provided a natural occasion for the Eucharist, but we have no direct evidence for it, and so that must remain in the realm of speculation. Equally speculative is the suggestion by Eligius Dekkers that it was the lateness of the hour that led to the transfer of the rite to the following morning,[31] as there is no specific evidence that it ended at a particularly late hour and if it had been of great length, it would have been equally difficult to accommodate it early on Sunday morning before the working day began. Other conceivable reasons for the shift include the possible existence of more widespread provincial bans on clubs of the type imposed by Pliny, which would have precluded an evening gathering, or a desire by Christians to dissociate their practice more sharply from Jewish Sabbath observance and to bring it into line with New Testament references to 'the first day of the week' understood in accordance with the Roman reckoning of the day. At least as far as north Africa is concerned, it appears possible that it may have been the practice of distributing communion from the reserved sacrament in the morning on station days that eventually encouraged full celebrations on Sunday mornings too.[32] Of course, it may have been a combination of factors rather than just one alone that was responsible for the ultimate universal adoption of the custom.

Justin may either be the earliest witness to this switch of practice, or he may not yet have known it: it all depends what he meant by 'the day called of the Sun' and whether we view the ministry of the word that he describes as a replica of the synagogue assembly, but now transferred to accompany the Eucharist, or another instance of the looser type developed in conjunction with the Eucharist such as we have outlined above. What Justin's account has in common with the Jewish practice is that both involve reading from honoured writings and an exposition of their meaning. Justin states that the Christian readings known to him consisted of 'the memoirs of the apostles or the writings of the prophets ... for as long as time allows'. But just what is the force of the conjunction 'or' here? Does it mean that the ministry of the word was so flexible in form that some weeks it might involve reading from the Old Testament (assuming that 'the writings of the prophets' is a generic description for the Jewish Scriptures as a whole rather than designating the prophetic books alone) but other weeks there would only be Christian texts?[33]

---

31 'L'église ancienne a-t-elle connu la messe du soir?', in *Miscellanea liturgica in honorem L. C. Mohlberg* I (Rome, 1948), pp. 233–57, here at p. 235.

32 See below, pp. 99–101.

33 M.-E. Boismard, *Le Diatessaron: de Tatien à Justin* (Paris, 1992), has argued that the 'records of the apostles' were an early gospel harmony rather than the New Testament writings as such.

Or does he describe it in this way because he knows of some communities that regularly include Old Testament readings but also of others that do not? Or should the conjunction be understood as really meaning 'and'? But if so, might not one have expected the Jewish Scriptures to have preceded the Christian writings, both in Justin's description and in the actual practice? Although many scholars have concluded that this is a direct descendent of the synagogue assembly, the nature of the description seems to suggest instead the sort of ministry of the word originally attached to the evening meal, and it may be significant that Rome is one of the places that later had no regular Old Testament reading in its eucharistic liturgy.

Justin's description of the 'common prayers' that follow the reading and exposition does little to help resolve the issue of the derivation of the first part of the service. Although I have suggested that praying might have been part of the synagogue practice, we have no actual evidence that it was so, but on the other hand, the New Testament allusions to ministries of the word held in conjunction with the Eucharist give no indication that prayers formed part of that element either. The fact that these common prayers continued to be included on a baptismal Sunday, even when the ministry of the word was apparently omitted,[34] might imply that they were viewed as an independent unit and not simply as the conclusion of that element. Could it be that they are simply one of the regular daily times of prayer expected of all Christians but celebrated in common on this occasion because the community happens to be gathered for another purpose anyway?[35]

The mutual greeting with a kiss that Justin describes as following the prayers on the occasion of a baptism does not seem to have been unique to that event, as it is attested as forming the conclusion of congregational prayer in several other sources from the end of the second century onwards, and so was almost certainly part of the liturgy on a regular Sunday, even though not explicitly mentioned as such by Justin. Dix regarded it as constituting the beginning of the second half of the Eucharist and thought that it was something inherited from Jewish practice,[36] but he appears to be wrong on both counts. The only earlier

---

34 Or was it not omitted after all, but merely preceded the baptism and/or continued during the time that the latter was being performed in another place, even though not explicitly mentioned by Justin?

35 On times of daily prayers, see Bradshaw, *Daily Prayer in the Early Church*, pp. 47–62, and the corrections to this in idem, *The Search for the Origins of Christian Worship*, pp. 175–6.

36 *The Shape of the Liturgy*, pp. 103–10.

evidence for such a custom is the reference in several of St Paul's letters to the exchange of a 'holy kiss' between Christians.[37] In the Graeco-Roman culture of the period, social convention usually restricted kissing to very close friends or members of one's own family, and hence for Christians to kiss one another when they were not so related was a powerful counter-cultural symbol, indicating that they regarded their fellow-believers as their brothers and sisters and the Church as their true family. This was reinforced, in some cases at least, by a consequent refusal to exchange kisses any longer with members of their natural family who were not themselves Christians.[38] Such behaviour would, of course, have been considered scandalous by outsiders.

From sevenfold to fourfold shape?

Dix's hypothesis concerning the origins of the Eucharist demanded that liturgical practice must have undergone a radical transformation from its earliest form to arrive at the pattern evidenced in Justin. According to him, an original sevenfold action over bread and cup separately would have been telescoped into a fourfold shape once the meal was eliminated and the elements brought together.[39] That, however, would have involved a diverse collection of local congregations all being willing to make the same major shift at about the same time, rather than choosing to preserve the distinctiveness of bread and cup rituals. On the other hand, if the more usual practice among Christians had always been to say thanksgivings over both cup and bread in immediate succession to one another at the very beginning of the meal, as in the *Didache* and possibly also other early sources,[40] then the disappearance of the meal or its reduction to merely symbolic proportions would not have necessitated any drastic change in practice to bring about the so-called fourfold shape of Justin and his successors. Indeed, it seems more than possible that Justin still expected separate prayers to be said over bread and cup one after the other, rather than a single prayer being said over both together. It is perhaps significant that he uses the plural, saying that the president 'sends up prayer*s* and thanksgiving*s* to the best of his ability' (67.5).[41] Even his next statement that 'the people assent, saying the

---

37 See L. Edward Phillips, *The Ritual Kiss in Early Christian Worship* (Nottingham, 1996), pp. 5–15.

38 See Michael Penn, 'Performing Family: Ritual Kissing and the Construction of Early Christian Kinship', *JECS* 10 (2002), pp. 151–74, especially 166–9.

39 See above, p. 12.

40 See above, pp. 24 and 43ff.

41 Mazza, *The Origins of the Eucharistic Prayer*, p. 60.

Amen' could mean that this was done after each prayer and not just once at the very end. In subsequent chapters I will note other evidence that supports the idea of the persistence of such separate prayer units rather than the early emergence of a single continuous composition,[42] which has been the dominant theory among liturgical scholars.

It is true that this particular instance seems to witness to a 'bread–cup' sequence rather than a 'cup–bread' one, as in the *Didache*, but that there might have been a difference in the order of thanksgivings in different Christian communities should not surprise us, especially as similar variations in the order of blessings, and disputes between different schools as to which one was correct, characterize a great deal of rabbinic literature. Thus, for example, the school of Shammai claimed that, even if wine was brought after the food, the blessing over the wine should still precede that over the food, while the school of Hillel said that the reverse was correct.[43] What both sequences – 'bread–cup' and 'cup–bread' – have in common is that the two thanksgivings would always have taken place in close proximity to one another at the beginning of the meal, and this practice would have continued unchanged even when a full meal was no longer included.

Wine or water?

Justin's account has usually been treated not only as the first clear exemplar of the 'classic' shape of the Eucharist but also as one involving what became the standard eucharistic elements – bread and wine. However, his testimony to the use of wine is not quite as unquestionable as it is generally presented. In 1891 Adolf von Harnack put forward the claim that the references to wine were interpolations and that the original text had referred to water alone.[44] Although this thesis has largely been ignored by subsequent scholars, attention has been drawn to it again recently by McGowan,[45] and it certainly deserves some consideration.

Harnack's case is that not only does Justin in his writings consistently compare the Eucharist to biblical and pagan meals involving water and never to those involving wine, but also in his description of the Last

---

42 See pp. 104–5 and 121–2.

43 Mishnah, *Ber.* 8.8. See ibid. 8.1–7 for other similar disputes over the order of blessings between these two rabbinic schools.

44 'Brod und Wasser: Die eucharistischen Elemente bei Justin', in *Über das gnostische Buch Pistis-Sophia; Brod und Wasser: die eucharistischen Elemente bei Justin. Zwei Untersuchungen* (Leipzig, 1891), pp. 115–44.

45 *Ascetic Eucharists*, pp. 151–5.

Supper in his *First Apology* 66.3 he refers simply to 'the cup', as he does elsewhere,[46] and again compares it to the Mithraic ritual use of bread and water. Furthermore, when in 65.3 wine is mentioned as being brought to the eucharistic president, there occurs the rather strange expression *hudatos kai kramatos*, literally 'water and wine-mixed-with-water'. Since *kai kramatos* was absent from one manuscript of the text, Codex Ottobianus, Harnack argued not only that it was an interpolation here but that in the two instances in 65.5 and 67.5 where the phrase 'bread and wine and water' occurs, the words 'and wine' had also been interpolated, even though the term used there was not *krama* but the more usual *oinos*.

Critics raised objections to Harnack's position on various grounds: that the reading of Codex Ottobianus was not to be trusted, that *krama* could simply mean 'wine', or that there were actually two separate cups, one of water and the other of wine mixed with water, as was evidenced for a baptismal Eucharist in some later sources.[47] Thus the arguments are not conclusive in one direction or the other, but McGowan believes that the case for water rather than wine is strengthened both by Justin's own roots in Asia and Syria, where water Eucharists were apparently widespread, and also by the known opposition to wine of his associate Tatian.[48] At the very least, Justin's account should be treated with some reserve on this particular point. It would certainly be ironic if the text constantly cited by scholars as the earliest description that we have of the 'conventional' Christian Eucharist turns out to have originally been describing one with water instead of wine.

---

46 See *Dialogue with Trypho* 41 and 70.
47 See McGowan, *Ascetic Eucharists*, pp. 151–5.
48 Ibid., pp. 155–9.

Chapter 5

Eucharistic Theology from Ignatius to Tertullian

As suggested in Chapter 3, eucharistic practice and theology in the second century were quite diverse in character, and the limited nature of the evidence makes it difficult to pursue every variety in detail. I must restrict myself here, therefore, to signs of an emerging theological consensus in the course of the century and attempt to trace its evolution.

The bloodless sacrifice

The early Christians were often accused of atheism by their pagan contemporaries because they appeared to lack the customary apparatus of a religion – temples, sacrifices and priests. As part of their response to this charge, Christian apologists insisted that they did still have sacrifices – but of a quite different kind. Thus Athenagoras in the second half of the second century argued that 'the Framer and Father of this universe does not need blood, nor the odour of burnt-offerings, nor the fragrance of flowers and incense', and he speaks of the 'bloodless sacrifice and spiritual worship' offered by Christians (*Plea for the Christians* 13), echoing in part Romans 12.1. A similar conjunction of the two terms is also found in the Jewish-Christian *Testament of Levi*, which was probably composed about the same period and talks of the 'spiritual and bloodless sacrifice' of heaven (3.6); and the expressions recur in many later Christian writings.[1]

What then was the sacrifice that Christians understood themselves to be offering? The New Testament concept that the primary oblation desired by God was a life of holiness is continued by second-century

---

1 See Kenneth W. Stevenson, '"The Unbloody Sacrifice": The Origins and Development of a Description of the Eucharist', in Gerard Austin (ed.), *Fountain of Life* (Washington, DC, 1991), pp. 103–30.

writers,[2] but alongside that can be seen the idea that acts of worship too may be described in this way. Thus Justin Martyr held that 'prayers and thanksgivings that are made by the worthy are the only perfect and pleasing sacrifices to God'.[3] Tertullian in north Africa at the end of the second century similarly asserted that Christians did 'sacrifice for the emperor's safety, but to our God and his, and in the way God commanded, by pure prayer' (*Ad Scap.* 2.8); he also describes their offering as 'the ascription of glory and blessing and praise and hymns' (*Adv. Marc.* 3.22.6) and 'simple prayer from a pure conscience' (ibid. 4.1.8); and he speaks of prayer as 'a spiritual victim (*hostia*) which has abolished the former sacrifices' and says that 'we sacrifice, in spirit, prayer – (a victim) proper and acceptable to God, which indeed he has required, which he has provided for himself. This (victim), devoted from the whole heart, fed on faith, tended by truth, entire in innocence, pure in chastity, garlanded with love, we ought to escort with a procession of good works, amid psalms and hymns, to God's altar, to obtain for us all things from God' (*De or.* 28; see also *Apol.* 30.5). Implicitly, therefore, these theologians were upholding the idea first found in Christian writings in the Letter to the Hebrews (13.15) and apparently drawn from the language of the Jewish community at Qumran, that words of worship, the 'fruit of the lips' (Hos. 6.2), could constitute the sacrifice of praise acceptable to God.[4]

The pure offering

As we saw in Chapter 2, the Eucharist was described as being a sacrifice as early as *Didache* 14. Nevertheless, a link was still maintained there to the New Testament understanding that it was the offering of the believer's life that constituted the primary Christian sacrifice through the application of Malachi 1.11, where the adjective 'pure' in that quotation was used to stress the moral integrity required of those who offered the sacrificial worship. The same quotation continued to be employed by later Christian writers, but with a polemical purpose, as part of their argument against Jews that it was Christian worship that was superior, because Scripture itself testified that it was the worship that was offered in every place by the Gentiles that was regarded as pure by God and not the worship offered in one place, the Temple, by Jews.

2 See the examples cited in Hanson, *Eucharistic Offering in the Early Church*, p. 6.
3 *Dialogue with Trypho* 117.2; see also his *First Apology* 13.1. On Justin's use of sacrificial language in general, see Lathrop, *Holy Things*, pp. 143–55.
4 See above, pp. 41–2.

We first encounter this use of the text in several places in Justin Martyr's *Dialogue with Trypho, a Jew* (28.5; 41.2; 116.3; 117.1). Justin also countered the argument that the text could be interpreted as meaning that while God had rejected the sacrifices of Jews in Jerusalem, he was still pleased with the prayers offered by Jews in the Diaspora. While, as we saw above, agreeing that 'prayers and thanksgivings that are made by the worthy are the only perfect and pleasing sacrifices to God', Justin denied that this applied to the Jews:

> because, first, not even now does your race exist from the rising to the setting of the sun, but there are nations in which none of your race ever lived – for there is not one single race of human beings, whether barbarians or Greeks, or by whatever name they may be called, or nomads, or vagrants, or herdsmen living in tents, among whom prayers and thanksgivings are not made through the name of the crucified Jesus to the Father and Maker of all – and then because, at that time when the prophet Malachi said this, your dispersion in all the earth, which now exists, had not taken place, as is also revealed from the scriptures. (117.3)

Irenaeus of Lyons later in the century continued in a similar vein to Justin. He asserted that the kind of offering had changed, in that it was not offered any more by slaves, that is, as an obligation, but by the free, that is, as a voluntary act (*Adv. haer.* 4.18.2). Malachi's prophecy demonstrated that 'the former people shall cease to offer to God' and their offering would be replaced by the pure sacrifice offered by Christians everywhere (ibid. 4.17.5), the 'name' that the prophecy said was to be glorified among the nations being none other than that of Jesus Christ, which God can call his own, 'both because it is (the name) of his Son and because he himself inscribing it, gave it for the salvation of humankind' (ibid. 4.17.6). Interestingly, both in Irenaeus' quotation of the text, and also once in Justin (*Dial.* 41.2), the word 'incense' is included, unlike the form in *Didache* 14 and elsewhere and in spite of its association with contemporary pagan worship and especially with the common test required of persecuted Christians that they offer incense to the Emperor. Irenaeus, however, added the comment that John in the Apocalypse had declared that 'incense' is 'the prayers of the saints' (*Adv. haer.* 4.17.6, referring to Rev. 5.8). For Irenaeus, Malachi's prophecy is not only directed against the Jews but also those Christians whom he regards as heretics, and so, like *Didache* 14, he insists that 'pure' sacrifice required the moral uprightness of those offering it. Indeed, he claimed that the sacrifice of Abel in Genesis was accepted by God, 'because he offered with singlemindedness and righteousness', while the offering of Cain was rejected, 'because with jealousy and malice he harboured in his heart division against his brother' and he concluded that 'sacrifices, therefore, do not sanctify a human being, for God does not need sacrifice, but the conscience of the one who offers, when it is pure, sanctifies the sacrifice' (*Adv. haer.* 4.18.3).

A comparable sentiment is expressed by Tertullian in *Adv. Marc.* 2.22.3, and by Cyprian in the middle of the third century in *De unit. eccl.* 13; while in *Adversus Iudaeos*, the attribution of which to Tertullian has sometimes been questioned, the Cain and Abel story is also employed in relation to Christian worship, but interpreted here as a foreshowing of a distinction between 'earthly oblations' and 'spiritual sacrifices': the elder son (Israel) offered earthly sacrifices, which were not accepted, but the younger son ('our people') offers spiritual sacrifices, which God receives, and which the prophets, including Malachi, revealed were to be offered in every place, and were defined as 'sacrifices of praise' and 'a contrite heart' (*Adv. Iud.* 5).

The oblation of bread and cup

Although most of these polemical arguments which made use of the Malachi text were referring to the Eucharist, too much significance should not be attached to that. Nor should one jump to the conclusion that the concept of sacrificial worship was limited to that rite alone, as early Christian writers were unanimous in arguing that it was prayer offered with righteous living that comprised their sacrifice of praise to God. Indeed, Origen, writing in the middle of the third century, claimed that the daily 'perpetual' sacrifices of the Old Testament found their true fulfilment in the perpetual prayer of Christians (see *Hom. in Num.* 23.3; *Contra Celsum* 8.21–2). Nevertheless, it would be natural for the Eucharist to come to be regarded as the supreme expression of prayer and thanksgiving.

Justin's writings go further than this, however. In his efforts to assert the superiority of Christianity over Judaism in his *Dialogue with Trypho*, he adduces not merely a spiritual counterpart and fulfilment of the Old Testament cult, but a material one too. Alongside his affirmation that prayers and thanksgivings were the only perfect and pleasing sacrifices to God, he asserts three times that Christ commanded Christians to *offer* the bread and cup of the Eucharist (41.1, 3; 70.4), describing this as being the sacrifice that fulfilled the prophecy of Malachi, and interpreting the offering of fine flour that had been prescribed under the old covenant on behalf of those purified from leprosy (Lev. 14.10) as the 'type' or prefiguration of the bread of the Eucharist. Although the verb used in the first occurrence and twice in the last one is *poiein*, literally 'to do', as in 'do this in my remembrance', it is a verb that can have cultic overtones, and the second occurrence confirms that meaning here by employing the more common verb for offer, *prospherein*, as well as the noun *thusia*, 'sacrifice', in relation to the bread and the cup.

Irenaeus followed Justin in seeking an Old Testament 'type' for the Eucharist, but he chose instead the offering of the first-fruits of creation (see, e.g., Deut. 26) and claimed that Christ 'gave instruction to his disciples to offer first-fruits to God from his own creatures', namely the bread and the cup of the Eucharist, 'which the church received from the apostles and offers throughout the whole world to God, who provides us with nourishment, the first-fruits of his gifts in the new covenant' (*Adv. haer.* 4.17.5). Because immediately before this statement he had just recalled the words of Jesus declaring the bread and cup to be his body and blood, some scholars have understood Irenaeus to be meaning that it is the body and blood of Jesus which are offered, but it seems more likely that he means that bread and cup are offered and that through this offering with thanksgiving they become the body and blood of Jesus.[5] Like Justin, he describes this as being the offering prophesied by Malachi. The image of the first-fruits had already been used in the New Testament of Christ, of the Spirit, and of the Church, and the Old Testament prescriptions had been applied in *Didache* 13 to justify the economic support of Christian prophets.[6] Irenaeus, however, seems to be the first to apply the idea explicitly to the eucharistic elements.[7] He appears to have selected this particular symbol because it affirmed not only the continuity of the God of the Old Testament and the God of the New but also the intrinsic goodness of created matter – both of these being fundamental planks in his argument against the dualism of his gnostic opponents. Thus, in commenting on the marriage feast at Cana, Irenaeus says that 'although the Lord could have provided wine for those feasting and filled with food those who were the hungry without using

---

5 See David N. Power, *Irenaeus of Lyons on Baptism and Eucharist* (Nottingham, 1991), p. 16, n. 1.

6 For these and for later Christian developments of the practice of offering first-fruits, see Paul F. Bradshaw, 'The Offering of the Firstfruits of Creation: An Historical Study', in Ralph McMichael, Jr (ed.), *Creation and Liturgy: Studies in Honor of H. Boone Porter* (Washington, DC, 1993), pp. 29–41.

7 But see Walter D. Ray, 'Toward a Narrative-Critical Approach to the Study of Early Liturgy', in Johnson and Phillips (eds), *Studia Liturgica Diversa*, pp. 3–30, esp. pp. 22ff., who tries to trace a line of development of this idea from the *Book of Jubilees* through *Didache* 9–10 to Irenaeus.

any pre-existent matter, he did not do so . . .' (*Adv. haer.* 3.11.5). Nevertheless, he continues to be insistent that Christians are to offer bread and cup in the Eucharist not as though God needed them, 'but that they themselves may be neither unfruitful nor ungrateful' (*Adv. haer.* 4.17.5; see also 4.18.1). In other words, as in *Adv. haer.* 4.18.3, quoted earlier, the prime value of the offering was still understood to lie in the opportunity it gave to worshippers to make a tangible articulation of their praise and thanksgiving rather than in any intrinsic effect the act itself conveyed.

What these two writers reveal is that, while the normal early Christian exegesis of the Old Testament was to look for spiritual counterparts for aspects of the cult, this was not carried through with complete consistency. Arguments against both Jewish and gnostic opponents could lead to material equivalents being adduced. This development will accelerate greatly in the fourth century and have profound consequences for eucharistic theology, even though both themes – the offering of praise and the offering of bread and cup – will continue to feature side by side even then.[8] The tendency to think of the bread and wine themselves forming the substance of the sacrifice rather than prayer and praise was no doubt encouraged, particularly after the full meal had been given up, by the continuing custom of the worshippers bringing those elements with them from their homes to be used in the Eucharist in just the same way as they also brought other things that were to be offered to God.[9] Thus we find the noun 'offering' (Greek, *prosphora*; Latin, *oblatio*) being regularly and unambiguously used by writers from beginning of the third century onwards to designate the bread and cup.[10] Justin's own adoption of a similar way of thinking may perhaps support the hypothesis that the Eucharist no longer included a full meal in his community.

Remembrance

Justin not only records Christ's command to 'do this in my remembrance' in his *First Apology* (66.3), but in his *Dialogue with Trypho* he is explicit that the Christian eucharistic sacrifice is offered 'in remem-

---

8 See below, pp. 147–52.
9 See Bradshaw, 'The Offering of the Firstfruits of Creation'.
10 For its use in Tertullian, see below, p. 101. The Syrian *Didascalia Apostolorum* speaks of a deacon standing by 'the offerings of the eucharist' (below, p. 104), and Cyprian criticizes the wealthy for coming to the Lord's Supper 'without a sacrifice' and hence taking a part of the sacrifice that the poor have offered (*De opere et eleemosynis* 15).

brance of the suffering which he underwent for the sake of those whose souls are cleansed from all wickedness' (41.1), the choice of the term 'cleansed' being a further allusion to the 'type' of the offering of fine flour in Leviticus 14.10, which he has just mentioned: just as that offering is fulfilled in the eucharistic bread, so too the cleansing of lepers for which it was made is fulfilled in the cleansing of Christians from all evil. And just as that earlier offering was a thanksgiving by the one who had been cleansed, so too Justin goes on to say that Christians make their offering 'so that we may at the same time give thanks to God for having created the world with all things in it for the sake of humanity, and for freeing us from the evil in which we were born, and utterly destroying the principalities and powers through him who suffered according to his will' (ibid.), probably alluding here to themes occurring in eucharistic prayers known to him.[11] In a subsequent passage, commenting on Isaiah 33.16 ('bread shall be given to him, and his water shall be sure'), he includes remembrance of Christ's incarnation along with his passion – indeed, he seems to give it greater prominence than the passion: this prophecy, he says, refers 'to the bread which our Christ commanded us to offer in remembrance of his being made flesh for the sake of those believing in him, for whom also he suffered; and to the cup which he commanded us to offer, giving thanks in remembrance of his blood' (70.4). He later returns to the subject once more and says that the remembrance is effected by believers' participation in 'their solid and liquid food, in which the suffering which the Son of God endured for us is remembered' (117.3).

In contrast, remembrance is not a major theme in Irenaeus' eucharistic theology. Nowhere in his writings does he explicitly link the offering of the eucharistic sacrifice to a memorial of the death of Christ. As Rowan Williams has noted, this is not particularly surprising, 'given Irenaeus' general lack of interest in the imagery of propitiation by bloodshed'.[12] But it does mean that second-century Christianity, at least as attested by its two great theological writers Justin and Irenaeus, does not seem to know the notion of 'memorial-sacrifice' as articulated by later theologians. For Justin the suffering of Christ is but one of several aspects remembered in the eucharistic sacrifice – and it is the suffering not the sacrificial death as such that is recalled – and Irenaeus does not think in those terms at all.

---

11 In his *First Apology* 13.2, he says that Christians ought 'to send up praises and hymns for our creation and all the means of health, the varieties of creatures and the changes of the seasons, and to send up petitions that we may live again in incorruption through faith in him'.

12 *Eucharistic Sacrifice – The Roots of a Metaphor* (Nottingham, 1982), p. 10.

Priesthood

Early Christians understood themselves not only to offer sacrifice in their worship but also to constitute a priesthood. Indeed, it is difficult to know which of the two images came first. Did they begin to see themselves as a priesthood because they thought of themselves as offering sacrifice, or was it because they viewed themselves as a priesthood that they came to regard their worship as a sacrifice offered to God? Or are the ideas so closely interrelated that such speculation is fruitless? Whatever the answer, the concept of the Christian Church as forming a priesthood is explicitly mentioned in several New Testament passages (1 Pet. 2.5, 9; Rev. 1.6; 5.10; 20.6), building on the image of Israel as intended to be a priesthood for the nations in Exodus 19.6, and it recurs in second-century writings. Thus Justin Martyr, referring once more to the Malachi prophecy to justify his claim, asserts that 'we are the true high priestly race of God, as even God himself bears witness, saying that in every place among the Gentiles they present to him pleasing and pure sacrifices. And God receives sacrifices from no one, except through his priests' (*Dialogue with Trypho* 116.3). Similarly, Irenaeus affirms that 'all the disciples of the Lord are Levites and priests' (*Adv. haer.* 5.34.3; see also ibid. 4.8.3), and Tertullian too speaks in sacerdotal terms of the whole Christian community (*De or.* 28.3), and likens post-baptismal anointing to the consecration of priests in the Old Testament (*De bapt.* 7).

This concept of Christians as being God's priestly people continued to leave its mark on later liturgical texts and practices, even though a different understanding of priesthood, of a ministerial priesthood within the Church, also began to emerge alongside it from the third century onwards. Of that idea, however, virtually no trace can be found in earlier sources. Indeed, Justin describes the chief minister within the Christian community neither as a priest (*hiereus*) nor even as an elder (*presbyteros*) or bishop (*episkopos*) but as the president (*proestos*) of the brethren (*First Apology* 65.3, 5; 67.4–6). T. G. Jalland suggested that he deliberately chose to use this generic expression as it was one that would be more intelligible to outsiders rather than the technical term 'bishop' regularly used by Christians.[13] L. W. Barnard responded, however, that Justin did not hesitate to use the word 'deacons' and that such terms were in any case not unknown to pagans; and he argued that because 'president' is found in *The Shepherd of Hermas* in connection with presbyters (*Vis.* 2.4; cf. *Vis.* 2.2; 3.9), it was used in the Roman Church at this time as a

---

13 'Justin Martyr and the President of the Eucharist', *SP* 5 (1962), pp. 83–5.

generic title to designate the chief officer of a community, who might be described either as a presbyter or a bishop by a particular group.[14] It could also be that Justin and others used this vague expression because other ministers too, especially Christian prophets, might still have assumed this role at the time.

Two early documents, however, do contain seeds of the later idea. *Didache* 13.3 likens Christian prophets to high-priests in a passage concerning the offering of first-fruits. But the motivation for this comparison appears to be economic rather than theological: prophets needed to receive material support if they were to be free to exercise their ministry, and hence the Old Testament commandments were invoked to justify the provision of that support by the Christian community. Similarly, the First Letter of Clement of Rome, usually dated around 96 CE, cites the example of the assignment of different liturgical roles to different ministers in the Old Testament Law (high-priests, priests, Levites, and people) as one of its principal arguments against Christians transgressing what the author regards as the appointed limits of their respective ranks (chs. 40—41), and also uses the cultic expression 'presented the gifts' in relation to Christian presbyter-bishops rather than to the Christian community as a whole (44.4). These passages, however, are unique within Christian literature of the first two centuries – there is, for example, no sign in our second-century Roman sources, Justin Martyr and *The Shepherd of Hermas*, of the kind of thinking evidenced in *1 Clement* – and in any case they do not go as far as explicitly saying that Christian ministers *are* priests. For that we have to wait until the beginning of the third century, when Tertullian – alongside his designation of the whole people as priestly – in one passage speaks of the bishop as high-priest, *summus sacerdos* (*De bapt.* 17.1), but elsewhere implies that 'priest' (*sacerdos*) may have already become a commonly used appellative for the bishop in the north African church (*De exhort. cast.* 7; 11; *De mon.* 12; *De pud.* 20.10; 21.17). Thereafter the use of such sacerdotal language for Christian ministers became standard.[15] One principal reason for this development is not hard to seek. Just as the disappearance of the meal seems to have encouraged the understanding of the bread and cup as being that which was offered in the Eucharist, so too the fact that the president no longer sat at table with the assembled community and prayed over the food that they were to eat together but stood apart from them and offered the gifts that they had brought to him cannot but have been a very significant factor in encouraging the use of sacerdo-

---

14 *Justin Martyr: His Life and Thought* (Cambridge, 1967), pp. 132–3.
15 For this development, see below, pp. 106, 108 and 111.

tal terms to describe his office and in seeing his ministry as a priesthood exercised on behalf of the people.

Eucharistic presence: Ignatius

While the letters written by Ignatius of Antioch early in the second century do not explicitly describe the Eucharist as a sacrifice, his use of the world 'altar' in apparent relation to the eucharistic assembly (*Eph.* 5.2; *Magn.* 7.2; *Phil.* 4; *Trall.* 7.2) has sometimes been thought to point in that direction.[16] Ignatius' direct sacrificial language is, not surprisingly, focused primarily on his impending martyrdom, but as he includes a eucharistic metaphor in that (*Rom.* 4.2: 'I am God's wheat and I am ground by the teeth of wild beasts so that I may be found pure bread of Christ'), it would seem to imply that he regarded the Eucharist as having a sacrificial character. What the letters certainly attest, however, is his conviction of the eucharistic presence of Christ. He views the bread not merely as having healing properties, describing it as 'the medicine of immortality and the antidote to dying' (*Eph.* 20.2), but as the body of Christ, or rather as the *flesh* of Christ: 'Take care, therefore, to have one Eucharist, for there is one flesh of our Lord Jesus Christ and one cup for union in his blood; one altar, as [there is] one bishop, with the presbytery and deacons, my fellow-servants; so that whatever you do, you do according to God' (*Phil.* 4). The author's choice of the word 'flesh' (*sarx*) here rather than 'body' (*soma*) reveals a greater affinity with the eucharistic thought of the Fourth Gospel than that of the Synoptics or Paul, which he shows no sign of knowing: 'The bread that I shall give for the life of the world is my flesh. . . . Unless you eat of the flesh of the Son of Man and drink his blood, you have no life in you' (John 6.51, 53). Thus Ignatius is stressing both the reality of Christ's incarnation and the reality of that same presence in the Eucharist.

The reason for this very strong emphasis and his equal insistence on the need for the unity of the Christian community in the one Lord becomes clearer in the light of the rest of his correspondence and in particular of his mention of the Eucharist again in his letter to the Smyrnaeans: 'They abstain from Eucharist and prayer, because they do not confess the Eucharist to be flesh of our Saviour Jesus Christ, which suffered for our sins, which the Father by his goodness raised up' (7.1). There has been some scholarly discussion as to how many different

---

16 But cf. William R. Schoedel, *Ignatius of Antioch* (Philadelphia, 1985), p. 21: 'the image of the altar . . . in Ignatius is not used to indicate the sacrificial character of the meal but to symbolize solidarity'.

types of Christians with whom he disagrees Ignatius is attacking in his various letters, but those he has in mind here are accused of having a docetic Christology, denying that Christ took flesh (see *Smyrn.* 5.2), and hence a defective eucharistic theology, denying that the elements are the flesh and blood of Christ. While in Ignatius' view these people are clearly heretics, it could be that they are in fact merely Christians with a more primitive Christology than his and a different eucharistic under-standing, in which the bread and cup were not identified with Christ's flesh, and so they were refusing to join in eucharistic celebrations which articulated doctrines that they did not espouse. That such groups of Christians were not simply abstaining from the Eucharist altogether but apparently holding their own assemblies is suggested in a later passage in the same letter:

> All (of you), follow the bishop, as Jesus Christ (does) the Father, and the presbytery as (you would) the apostles; and reverence the deacons, as the commandment of God. Let no one do anything connected with the church without the bishop. Let that be con-sidered a proper Eucharist, which is (administered) either by the bishop, or by one to whom he has entrusted (it). Wherever the bishop shall appear, there let the multitude be; just as, wherever Jesus Christ is, there is the catholic church. It is not permitted without the bishop either to baptize or to hold an *agape*; but whatever he shall approve, that is also pleasing to God, so that everything that you do may be secure and valid. (*Smyrn.* 8)

The picture painted by this and other appeals to unity scattered throughout the letters of Ignatius suggests a situation where there were at least two if not more rival gatherings of Christians in a particular locality, one accepting the authority of the bishop and holding a 'high' doctrine of eucharistic presence, and at least one other with its own leaders and a eucharistic celebration that was perhaps more akin in form and theology to that behind *Didache* 9—10. It is small wonder then that appeals to unity pepper Ignatius' correspondence as he struggled to assert the primacy of episcopal authority over disparate groups of Christians.[17]

---

17 See further Christine Trevett, 'Prophecy and Anti-episcopal Activity: A Third Error Combatted by Ignatius?', *JEH* 34 (1983), pp. 1–18.

Eucharistic presence: Justin and Irenaeus

Justin Martyr is equally convinced of the eucharistic presence of Christ:

> For not as common bread or common drink do we receive these things; but just as our Saviour Jesus Christ, being incarnate through (the) word of God, took both flesh and blood for our salvation, so too we have been taught that the food over which thanks have been given through (a) word of prayer which is from him, from which our blood and flesh are fed by transformation, is both the flesh and blood of that incarnate Jesus.[18]

Notice has hardly ever been taken by scholars of the fact that Justin, like Ignatius of Antioch and also the Gospel of John, speaks of 'flesh' rather than 'body' here,[19] but it does suggest that all three are reflecting an early theological tradition that originally did not know the sayings of Jesus about body and blood, as inserted into the Last Supper narratives of the Synoptic Gospels and lying behind the account in 1 Corinthians 11, but instead referred to the eucharistic food as the flesh and blood of Christ.

However, it appears that in this particular instance there has been a confluence of the two traditions, since immediately afterwards Justin does quote the sayings about the bread and cup being body and blood. Nevertheless, he shows no awareness of the context in which these sayings are found in the New Testament, and so the 'body and blood' language is no more directly linked with the passion and death of Christ than is the 'flesh and blood' language: it is seemingly not his dead body, his sacrificed body, that is in mind but his incarnate body, his living body: the bread and cup become the flesh and blood of the incarnate Jesus in order to feed and transform the flesh and blood of believers – his life enables their new life. As I observed in Chapter 1, in the *First Apology* there is no reference to the occasion on which Jesus spoke the words, to the Supper itself or to the interpretative words connecting body and blood to the covenant.[20] This last omission might be thought to be accounted for by the fact that Justin was speaking to pagans with no understanding of the biblical covenant relationship, but as Ratcliff

---

18 *First Apology* 66.2. For the full context of this extract, see above, p. 62.
19 Rare exceptions include Ratcliff, 'The Eucharistic Institution Narrative of Justin Martyr's *First Apology*', p. 102 (46); R. D. Richardson, 'A Further Enquiry into Eucharistic Origins with Special Reference to New Testament Problems', in Lietzmann, *Mass and Lord's Supper* (1978 edn), pp. 217–699, here at pp. 240–1.
20 See above, p. 15.

pointed out, even in his *Dialogue with Trypho*, where there is much anti-Jewish polemic concerning the old and new covenants, Justin never once uses the expression, 'the blood of the covenant'.[21] It is true that, as we saw earlier in this chapter, in the *Dialogue* Justin does say that Christ's suffering is one of the things in remembrance of which the eucharistic sacrifice is offered (41.1), but no greater emphasis is placed on that than on thanksgiving for creation or Christ's incarnation. Indeed, I noted that in 70.4 the incarnation even seems to take precedence over the passion: the bread is 'in remembrance of his being made flesh for the sake of those believing in him, for whom also he suffered'.

I observed in Chapter 1 that in his account of the body and blood sayings Justin uses *homoios*, 'similarly', instead of the Lukan and Pauline equivalent, *hosautos*.[22] R. D. Richardson pointed to this as one of several further possible signs of a link between Justin's tradition and the Fourth Gospel: the word also turns up in the account of the miraculous feeding of the multitude with loaves and fishes in John 6.11, where again, as in the case of Justin, there is no reference to the breaking of the bread but only to taking, thanking and distributing; and it is later in the same chapter of John's Gospel of course that the discourse about the bread of life and the necessity to eat the flesh and drink the blood of the Son of man occurs.[23] This is not to suggest that Justin was familiar with this part of John's Gospel as such but rather that the tradition he had received about the bread and cup being the flesh and blood of Christ may have been linked to the same feeding story as in John, and that knowledge of this story may perhaps have had some influence on the way in which the sayings about body and blood were also recounted.

It may be wondered how this tradition could have persisted in ignoring the association of the sayings over bread and cup with Christ's sacrificial death that is made both in the Synoptic Gospels and in 1 Corinthians once these writings began to be more widely known. It needs to be remembered, however, how little influence the Pauline theology of baptism as dying and rising with Christ played upon the early Christian – and especially Eastern – understanding of Christian initiation prior to the fourth century, even though Romans 6 was well known.[24] In the light of this, it perhaps appears less remarkable that at

---

21 Ratcliff, 'The Eucharistic Institution Narrative of Justin Martyr's *First Apology*', p. 102 (46).
22 See p. 16. He also uses this same link word in his reference to the bread and cup of the eucharist in *Dialogue* 41.3.
23 'A Further Enquiry into Eucharistic Origins', p. 241.
24 See Maxwell E. Johnson, *The Rites of Christian Initiation* (Collegeville, 1999), pp. 57–8.

least some Christian thinking about eucharistic presence in the first and second centuries also continued to follow what might be described as Johannine rather than Synoptic or Pauline paths.

By the time of Irenaeus later in the century, however, things were beginning to change. The written narratives of the New Testament were now starting to exercise greater influence over the eucharistic language of the oral catechetical traditions – a process I examined in Chapter 1. Hence, although (as we saw there) Irenaeus appears to know a similar form of the sayings tradition to Justin, he consistently uses 'body and blood' language in reference to the eucharistic presence and not 'flesh and blood'. Nonetheless, even though he also cites part of the Matthean version of the Last Supper narrative (*Adv. haer.* 5.33.1), it is upon its eschatological statement about drinking in the kingdom that he comments, passing over in silence the reference to the 'blood of the new covenant, which will be poured out for many for forgiveness of sins'. Thus, there is still nothing to suggest that the thinking of Paul or the Synoptics was as yet having a major impact on eucharistic theologies of the time. Although at one point Irenaeus does move from mention of redemption with the blood of the Lord to the cup of the Eucharist as being communion in his blood (ibid. 5.2.2), he does not develop the link further but, like Justin, sees the eucharistic body and blood of Jesus primarily in terms of nourishment for human flesh and so giving it the hope of resurrection to eternal life (ibid. 4.18.5; 5.2.3) rather than as that which was sacrificed for human salvation.

Consecration

Justin is the first Christian writer to put forward what might be called a theory of consecration, describing a change in the bread and cup. He takes the usually intransitive verb *eucharistein*, 'to give thanks', and employs it three times in his *First Apology* (65.5, 66.2 and 67.5), in a passive participle translated above in Chapter 4 as 'over which thanks have been given', although its sense might be better rendered by 'eucharistized'. Greek does have a verb to express the notion of 'sanctify' or 'consecrate', *hagiazein*, which Justin could have used here and which does appear a number of times in the New Testament. Thus his preference for *eucharistein* demonstrates how dominant the concept of thanksgiving as the primary action of the Eucharist still was, even though a movement towards understanding it also as involving an effect upon the material elements had already begun. This in turn seems to have led to the word *eucharistia* already being used to denote to the 'eucharistized' food rather than to the rite as a whole (66.1). Just what the rite itself might have been called in his circle Justin does not say.

He then goes on to describe how he believes this change is brought about: 'through (a) word of prayer which is from him' (66.2); but it is not clear whether this is part of what he says 'we have been taught' or not, or indeed exactly how it should be translated. G. J. Cuming argued that, while other interpretations could not be ruled out completely, the most likely rendering was 'by the prayer of the form of words which is from him [i.e., Jesus]', believing the 'form of words' in the prayer to be the institution narrative quoted in the very next sentence.[25] Anthony Gelston challenged Cuming's arguments and proposed that the phrase ought instead to be rendered 'through a word of prayer that is from him [i.e., Jesus]', and meant that consecration was effected 'through a prayer of thanksgiving offered in conformity with the pattern of Jesus' thanksgiving at the Last Supper'. Gelston rejected the idea that there would have been any fixed formula in use at that early period and drew attention to a somewhat similar expression in 1 Timothy 4.5 regarding 'clean' and 'unclean' food: 'For everything created by God is good, and nothing is to be rejected if it is received with thanksgiving; for then it is consecrated (*hagiazetai*) by the word of God and prayer.' Although biblical commentators have been divided over the precise meaning of 'word' in this verse (Scripture that was cited in the prayer itself or the word at the beginning of creation?), yet Gelston believed that, whatever the correct exegesis, it provided some sort of parallel to Justin's statement.[26]

Subsequent scholars have generally followed either one or other opinion of these two scholars, but Michael Heintz has recently suggested an alternative translation of the phrase: 'through the prayer of the Word which is from him [i.e., God]'. He justifies this reading on the basis of the parallelism that he sees set out in the passage between the incarnation effected *dia logou* and the food eucharistized *dia logou*, implying that in both cases *logou* here means 'the Word' and not simply 'a word', and hence the 'him' at the end of the phrase refers to God.[27]

Heintz is undoubtedly correct in recognizing that an intentional parallel is being drawn by Justin between the process of incarnation and of eucharistic consecration here, just as Ignatius had earlier insisted on the equivalent reality of Christ's incarnation and of his eucharistic

---

25 'Δι' ΕΥΧΗΣ ΛΟΓΟΥ (Justin, *Apology*, i.66.2)', *JTS* 31 (1980), pp. 80–2.
26 'Δι' ΕΥΧΗΣ ΛΟΓΟΥ (Justin, *Apology* i.66.2)', *JTS* 33 (1982), pp. 172–5.
27 'δι' εὐχῆς λόγου παρ ' αὐτοῦ (Justin, *Apology* 1.66.2): Cuming and Gelston Revisited', *SL* 33 (2003), pp. 33–6. The parallelism of these phrases had been noted earlier by S. Agrelo, 'El "Logos" divina que hace la eucaristía. Testimonio de san Justino', *Antonianum* 60 (1985), pp. 602–63.

presence.[28] This not only explains why in *Dialogue* 70.4 Justin regards the eucharistic bread as a remembrance especially of the incarnation, but also increases the likelihood that the word *logou* does mean the same in both instances. Moreover, the liturgical evidence of the period provides no greater support for Gelston's interpretation of the phrase than it does for Cuming's: just as there is nothing to suggest that the narrative of institution found a place in eucharistic prayers before the fourth century, so too there is no indication that eucharistic thanksgivings were patterned in any distinctive way after the model of Jesus but rather assumed diverse forms. Even 1 Timothy 4.5 appears to favour Heintz's thesis more than Gelston's. It is improbable that 'the word of God' in this verse really does mean Old Testament quotations incorporated into prayer-texts, since once again there is no evidence that this was being consciously done on a regular basis either by Jews or by Christians at this early period, but rather that the language of prayer naturally included echoes of biblical phrases. Thus the expression is probably best understood as referring to the word of God in creation – or the Logos, as Justin would have said. Indeed, Justin's phrase may simply be an elision of the twofold concept of the source of sanctification found in 1 Timothy – the word of God and prayer. If so, it implies that Justin was developing the notion that the principal agent of eucharistic consecration was the Logos and thus, as Heintz conjectures at the end of his essay, building a foundation for the invocation of the Logos that we find in a number of later texts.

Epiclesis

Although Irenaeus in two passages does employ similar expressions to Justin with regard to eucharistic consecration, using the phrases 'to eucharistize cups' (*Adv. haer.* 1.13.2) and 'eucharistized bread' (ibid. 4.18.4), and in another passage appears to associate thanksgiving with sanctification (ibid. 4.18.6: 'we offer to God . . . giving thanks for his gift and sanctifying what has been created'), yet his preference seems to be to introduce a different Greek word into the vocabulary associated with this idea – *epiklesis*, 'invocation'. He uses this expression in his description of the heretical activities of the Valentinian gnostic Marcus, who 'pretending to eucharistize cups mixed with wine, and protracting to great length the word of invocation, makes them appear purple and reddish' (ibid. 1.13.2). But he also applies it to the orthodox process of consecration: 'as bread from the earth, receiving the invocation of God,

---

28 See above, p. 87.

is no longer common bread but eucharist, consisting of two realities, earthly and heavenly, so also our bodies, receiving the eucharist, are no longer corruptible, having the hope of the resurrection to eternity' (ibid. 4.18.5). In another place he adopts a variant of this idea: 'the cup that has been mixed and the bread that has been made receive the word of God and become the eucharist of Christ's body and blood' (ibid. 5.2.3). Like Justin, he employs the word 'eucharist' to denote the consecrated elements rather than the rite, but unlike Justin, he appears to associate the consecration with the petitionary rather than the praise element of prayer. Although these passages do not necessarily mean that Irenaeus was already familiar with an explicit liturgical formula invoking the Logos within the prayer itself,[29] yet they certainly lay the groundwork for the sort of formulae we find in later sources, as we shall see in Chapter 8.

Eucharistic presence: Tertullian

Tertullian speaks in similar realistic terms of the eucharistic elements as do the earlier writers, declaring that the bread is the Lord's body (e.g., *De or.* 19; *De idol.* 7) and that human flesh feeds on the body and blood of Christ in order that the soul may be fattened on God (*De res. carn.* 8.3). On the other hand, in his controversy with Marcion, where he is concerned to argue the reality of Christ's incarnate body against his opponent's docetism, he instead makes use of the noun *figura*, 'figure', and its related verb *figurare* in relation to body and blood in two passages. First, in seeking to expound the meaning of the Septuagint text of Jeremiah 11.19, 'Come, let us cast wood on his bread', he says that bread here signifies body. 'For thus did God also in your own gospel[30] reveal it, calling bread his body, so that thereby you may understand that he has given to bread the figure of his body, whose body the prophet formerly represented (*figuravit*) as bread, while the Lord himself would subsequently interpret this mystery (*sacramentum*)' (*Adv. Marc.* 3.19.3–4). He returns to this same supposed prophecy of the Passion later in the work:

> Having taken bread and given it to the disciples, he made it his body by saying, 'This is my body', that is, the figure of my body. A figure, however, there could not have been, unless there were a real body. An empty thing, or phantom, is incapable of a figure. On

---

29 See S. Agrelo, 'Epiclesis y eucaristía en S. Ireneo', *EO* 3 (1986), pp. 7–27.
30 I.e. Luke, the only Gospel accepted by the Marcionites.

the other hand, if he pretended the bread was his body, because he lacked a real body, he must therefore have handed over bread for us. It would support Marcion's docetism (*vanitatem*) for bread to have been crucified! But why would he call his body bread, and not rather a melon, which Marcion must have had in place of a heart? He did not understand how ancient was this figure of the body of Christ, who said through Jeremiah: 'They have plotted against me, saying, Come, let us cast wood on his bread', meaning the cross on his body. And thus the illuminator of the ancient (prophecies) declared plainly what he had then wished the bread to mean when he called the bread his body. Similarly, when mentioning the cup and making the covenant to be sealed by his blood, he confirms the reality of his body. For blood can belong to no body except one of flesh. For if an unfleshly kind of body were set before us, unless it were fleshly, it would certainly not have blood. Thus, proof of the body depends on the evidence of the flesh, proof of the flesh on the evidence of the blood. (ibid. 4.40.3–4)

He then goes on to quote the use of wine as a figure for blood in Isaiah 63 and in Genesis 49.11, and concludes: 'Thus he has now also consecrated his blood in the wine who then represented the wine as [literally: in] the blood.'

Taking these passages together, the meaning of *figura* for Tertullian in this context is clear. Just as bread and wine in the Old Testament texts are seen as prophetic prefigurations of the body and blood of Christ, so too were the bread and wine that Jesus took at the Last Supper. It is important to note, however, that Tertullian is here speaking about the Last Supper and he does not say that the bread and wine of the Christian Eucharist are also to be understood in terms of *figura*. Whatever may have been the usage of the word by later writers,[31] such a conclusion does not necessarily follow, any more than Tertullian's apparent belief that it was the words of Jesus that made the bread his body at the Last Supper ('he made it his body by saying, "This is my body"') means that he also believed that it was necessary for these words to be recited in the Christian Eucharist in order to consecrate the bread. This is where debates between Catholics and Protestants over the meaning of *figura* in Tertullian have generally missed the mark.

---

31 For that usage, see Victor Saxer, 'Figura corporis et sanguinis Domini: une formule eucharistique des premiers siècles chez Tertullien, Hippolyte et Ambroise', *Rivista di archeologia cristiana* 47 (1971), pp. 65–89.

On the other hand, two other points should also be noted about the passage quoted above. First, unlike most earlier Christian writers, Tertullian does make an explicit link between Jesus' words over bread and cup and the Passion, and especially connects the cup with 'the covenant to be sealed by his blood'. He thus implies that the New Testament narratives are at last beginning to shape eucharistic theology. Second, he uses the language of 'consecrate' in relation to the wine, and not only here ('he has now also consecrated his blood in the wine') but also in *De anima* 17.13 ('wine which he consecrated in memory of his blood'). He gives no clearer indication as to what he meant by this word, however, nor – unlike his predecessors Justin and Irenaeus – how he thought the consecration was effected, although the *De anima* quotation may imply that he recognized some sort of distinction existing between the blood of Christ shed on the cross and what was consecrated in the cup. To this passage we may add *Adv. Marc.* 1.14, where Tertullian uses the word *repraesentat* when speaking of the relationship between the eucharistic bread and Christ's body. On the basis of his use of this verb and its associated noun *repraesentatio* in other contexts,[32] 'manifests' might be a better translation here than 'represents'. Beyond this, however, it is impossible to go in expounding his theology of eucharistic presence. For we cannot expect to obtain precision in answers to questions that the ancient authors do not appear to have asked themselves.

---

32 See the examples cited in Dix, *The Shape of the Liturgy*, pp. 255–6.

Chapter 6

The Eucharist in the Third Century

The evidence presented by the various third-century sources with regard to eucharistic theology and practice may be a little more plentiful than that offered in the second century, but it still leaves considerable gaps in our knowledge. Our principal witnesses come from just three regions – Alexandria, north Africa and Syria – and span the period from the very beginning of the century to its middle. The church order known as the *Apostolic Tradition* has not been included here as an independent source for the Eucharist at Rome since the provenances and dates of its contents are so much in doubt. However, reference is made to it at points where it offers a possible parallel to something mentioned in one of the other witnesses.

North Africa: Tertullian

In addition to insights into his eucharistic theology, which I examined in the previous chapter, Tertullian also provides some limited evidence for the eucharistic practices of his region. In defending the propriety of the activities of Christians against the charges of scandalous behaviour that were brought against them by pagans, he offers an indication in his *Apology*, written just before the end of the second century, as to what went on in their liturgical gatherings:

> We gather in an assembly and congregation, so that we may surround God with prayers, as if with united force. This violence is pleasing to God. We also pray for the emperors, for their ministers and authorities, for the state of the age, for the peace of the world, for the delay of the end. We meet for the recollection of our sacred writings, in case any aspect of the present times serves either to forewarn or to remind. Certainly, we nourish our faith with the sacred words, we arouse our hope, we strengthen our trust; and at

the same time by inculcating the precepts we confirm good habits. In the same place also there are exhortations, chastisements, and sacred censures. For with great gravity one is judged, as is fitting among those certain that they are in the sight of God; and the greatest anticipation of the future judgment occurs when any one has sinned to such an extent as to be excluded from participation in prayer, the assembly, and all sacred intercourse. Approved elders preside over us, having attained that honour not by purchase, but by testimony, for none of the things of God is bought with money. Although there is a treasure-chest, it is not filled with purchase-money, as of a religion that was bought. Once a month or whenever they desire, everyone puts in a small donation, but only if they wish and only if they are able; for no one is compelled, but contributes voluntarily. These are, as it were, the deposits of piety. For they are not spent from there on banquets and drinking parties and eating-houses, but on feeding and burying the poor, on boys and girls destitute of means and parents, and on the elderly now confined to the house, likewise the shipwrecked; and any in the mines, on the islands, or in prisons, provided that it is for belonging to the cause of God, become the foster-children of their confession. (*Apol.* 39)

Thus we learn, not to our surprise, that these meetings included Scripture-reading, homilies, prayers, the exercise of discipline and charitable giving. But we do not know from this whether what is being described is a eucharistic assembly or merely a service of the word on its own, which we learn from one other passage did exist in Tertullian's church.[1] Later in the same chapter, however, he describes a Christian supper:

Our supper reveals its meaning by the name that it is called among the Greeks, affection [*agape*]. Whatever it costs, our expenditure is gain in the name of piety, since with that feast we assist any in need; not as among you parasites, who strive for the glory of serving their licentiousness while filling their bellies amidst outrageous behaviour; but as with God, there a great respect for the lowly. If the reason for our feast is honourable, consider the rest of its ordering: as it is an act of religious duty, it permits no vileness or immodesty; no one reclines before prayer to God is first tasted; as much is eaten as satisfies those who are hungry, as much is drunk

---

1 *De cult. fem.* 2.11, where he states that 'either the sacrifice is offered or the word of God is dispensed'.

as is appropriate for the chaste. They are satisfied with that, as those who remember that even during the night they have to worship God; they converse as those who know that the Lord is listening. After the washing of hands and (the bringing in of) lights, each is invited into the midst to sing to God, as they are able, either from the holy scriptures or of their own composition: this proves how little is drunk. Prayer similarly concludes the feast. We depart from it, not as troops of mischief-doers nor bands of vagabonds, nor for outbursts of licentiousness, but (to have) the same care of our modesty and chastity as those who had gathered not so much for a banquet as for instruction. (ibid.)

Is this a eucharistic celebration? Most scholars have rapidly concluded that it is not, because of Tertullian's reference to the term *agape* in describing it, but as we have seen earlier,[2] that appellation was actually used by Christians in the first two centuries to denote a eucharistic meal. In any case, what else might we expect him to call the Eucharist? Like other writers of the period, he uses the word 'Eucharist' to refer to the eucharistic bread itself, and even the other synonyms he does employ for the rite seem more apposite to an evening meal than to some other kind of occasion ('the Lord's Supper', *De spect.* 13; 'the Lord's banquet', *Ad uxor.* 2.4; 'God's banquet', *Ad uxor.* 2.8). Moreover, the gathering involves prayer at the beginning and the end, moderate eating and drinking, the singing of religious songs, and concern for those in need – all characteristics of earlier Christian eucharistic meals – and is even described by Tertullian as 'an act of religious duty' (*officio religionis*). Thus on the basis of this, Andrew McGowan would claim that a eucharistic celebration in the context of an evening meal was still the practice in north Africa at this time.[3]

What, then, are we to make of Tertullian's statement in a work written about ten to fifteen years later, that 'we take also in gatherings before daybreak and from the hand of none but the presidents the sacrament of the Eucharist, which was commanded by the Lord both (to be) at meal-times and (to be taken) by all' (*De cor.* 3)? Does this not demonstrate that the celebration of the Eucharist had been transferred from the evening supper to the early morning? The practice cannot have been recent innovation, as it forms part of a list of customs that Tertullian says arise from tradition rather than Scripture. McGowan, however, suggests

---

2 Above, pp. 29–30.
3 See Andrew B. McGowan, 'Rethinking Agape and Eucharist in Early North African Christianity', *SL* 34 (2004), pp. 165–76.

that this passage is referring instead to the act of receiving communion from elements consecrated at a preceding evening meal. We know from another passage in Tertullian's works that the faithful might take the consecrated bread home and consume it there, presumably on days when there was no eucharistic celebration, because he warns that this practice may be a problem for a woman married to an unbeliever: 'Will not your husband know what you secretly taste before (taking) any food? And if he knows (it is) bread, does he not believe it to be that which it is said (to be)? And will any (husband), not knowing the reason for these things, simply endure them, without complaint, without suspicion of (whether it is) bread or poison?' (*Ad uxor.* 2.5). However, what is being referred to in the earlier passage is clearly something different from this domestic custom, as it is said to be received 'from the hand of . . . the presidents'. It may be a congregational version of such communion, held on what were known as 'station days' – the regular Wednesday and Friday fast days each week. Tertullian again offers evidence for some sort of eucharistic gatherings on these days in his treatise on prayer, when he attempts to counter what was apparently a widespread objection to participation in these assemblies, raised on the grounds that reception of the eucharistic bread would break the fast. Tertullian proposes the solution that people should attend the gathering but reserve the sacrament for later consumption, thus fulfilling both aspects of the day, worship and fasting:

> Similarly also on station days, many do not think that they should attend the sacrificial prayers, because the station would be undone by receiving the Lord's body. Does then the Eucharist destroy a service devoted to God or bind it more to God? Surely your station will be more solemn if you have also stood at God's altar? If the Lord's body is received and reserved, each point is secured, both the participation in the sacrifice and the discharge of the duty. (*De or.* 19)

But what sort of liturgical assembly was this? Although the language used here ('sacrificial prayers', 'God's altar', 'the sacrifice') might suggest that a eucharistic celebration was taking place, McGowan believes that such words and phrases are quite consistent with Tertullian's language about prayer in general,[4] and that therefore this need not indicate a full eucharistic rite but rather the distribution of consecrated bread at the conclusion of a morning gathering for prayer or for a service of the word. It can hardly be the liturgical assembly that Tertullian implies in

---

4 See similar examples above, p. 79.

his treatise on fasting (*De ieiun.* 10) took place on station days at the ninth hour, that is, around 3 p.m., for the fast usually ended at that point in the day and so eucharistic reception would have been no problem.

If McGowan is right, Tertullian provides testimony that not only was it possible for the reception of communion to take place at home by those who had been present at the rite as well as by those prevented from being there, but that such a distribution could now happen also in more formal community gatherings.[5] This implies that the act of eating Christ's body and drinking his blood was regarded as of such central importance by worshippers at this period that it was thought acceptable for it be divorced from the rest of the rite, a view that seems to be confirmed by Cyprian's language later, as we shall see. At the same time, however, we are perhaps also witnessing the beginning of a further process of separation that will later take hold everywhere – the severing of the celebration of the Eucharist from its earlier intrinsic connection with the Lord's day. Tertullian has generally been thought to provide the earliest evidence for the celebration of the Eucharist on the feast days of martyrs. As part of the same list of traditional practices in *De corona*, he says that 'we make offerings (*oblationes . . . facimus*) for the departed, for their birthdays on the anniversary' (the term 'birthday' being commonly used by early Christians to denote the day of a martyr's death, as being their birth into eternal life). On the other hand, Eoin de Bhaldraithe has challenged the normal interpretation of this text.[6] Drawing on a study made by Rupert Berger of the use of the terms *offerre* and *oblatio* in Tertullian, which indicated that the verb *offerre*, when used in connection with the Eucharist, could mean to prepare for the celebration, to buy food and place it on the table,[7] de Bhaldaithe concludes that Tertullian does not mean that the Eucharist itself was offered on the actual anniversary, but only that the *oblatio* was prepared then, that is, the bread was baked, and then the offering was made at the normal communal celebration on the following Sunday. Although he has to admit that Tertullian in one other passage does explicitly say 'offers on the anniversary' (*De monog.* 10), he believes that this must be a shorthand designation for 'prepares the offerings'.

---

5 We should also note that Eusebius records that Irenaeus, in discussion with Pope Victor in Rome at the end of the second century, affirmed that consecrated bread had traditionally been sent from one church to others (*Hist. eccl.* 5.24.15).

6 '*Oblationes pro defunctis, pro nataliciis annua die facimus*. What did Tertullian mean?', *SP* 20 (1989), pp. 346–51.

7 *Die Wendung 'offerre pro' in der römischen Liturgie* (Münster 1965), pp. 29–32, 42–60, and especially p. 44, section 3.

Beyond the passages examined above, however, Tertullian provides very little indication as to the form or contents of the eucharistic rite as it was known to him. Earlier scholars have often failed to distinguish references in Tertullian's writings to elements of Christian worship that seem to have taken place in private or at services of the word or are simply ambiguous as regards their context from those that are explicitly said to have been part of the Eucharist, and hence have assumed that we know more details of that rite than we can be certain that we do. So, for example, *Apol.* 22 speaks of the works of the prophets being read aloud and *De praescript.* 36 says that the writings of the apostles are read, but neither passage makes it clear whether these practices belong to the Eucharist or only to the separate service of the word. Similarly, both *Ad uxor.* 2.8 and *De or.* 27 mention psalms being sung, but the former probably refers to a domestic setting and the latter concerns the practice of daily prayer rather than the eucharistic liturgy. On the other hand, while other references to psalm-singing in Tertullian's writings (*De exhort. cast.* 10; *De spect.* 25 and 29; *De or.* 28) are not specific about the context in which it happens, both *Apol.* 39 quoted earlier in this chapter and *De ieiun.* 13 clearly refer to psalms being sung at the supper.

Other allusions to liturgical practices are also ambiguous. There appears to be a description of the order of the liturgy of the word in *De anima* 9.4, which speaks of a Montanist woman, 'a sister among us', seeing visions, 'while the scriptures are being read, or psalms sung, or sermons preached, or prayers made'. This happens, Tertullian says, 'in the church amid the solemnities of the Lord's day', but whether this is part of a eucharistic liturgy that is being described or a separate service of the word that might have taken place then we cannot say for sure. *De praescript.* 41 speaks of heretics who do not separate catechumens from believers, or even the heathen, but all alike listen and pray together, thus clearly implying that in 'orthodox' congregations the ministry of the word (or at least some part of it[8]) and the prayers that followed were restricted to the baptized alone – but once again it is not clear whether this relates to the Eucharist or to a service of the word. We do know that among the objects of intercession were the Emperor (see *Ad Scap.* 2.8; *Apol.* 30, 32 and 39) and enemies and persecutors (*De or.* 29), and that prayer was apparently concluded by the exchange of a kiss, which Tertullian describes as forming 'the seal of prayer' (*De or.* 18). In this last passage he is criticizing those who refuse to join in the kiss when

8 Apparently the Gospel reading: see Bradshaw, 'The Gospel and the Catechumenate in the Third Century'.

keeping a personal fast, presumably because they thought that the exchange would break the fast. But Tertullian objects that by their refusal they are revealing that they are fasting and thereby offending against Christ's precept that they should fast in secret (Matt. 6.17–18).[9] It is highly unlikely that the particular reference here is to a day on which the Eucharist was being celebrated, because Tertullian indicates elsewhere that such days were not ones on which any fasting was permitted (*De cor.* 3). Nevertheless, if prayer was normally concluded by a kiss on other occasions, there seems no reason to suppose that the same practice might not have obtained at eucharistic celebrations as well. Finally, we may note that *De idol.* 7 indicates that communion was received in the hand, and *De cor.* 3 refers to the care taken not to let any wine or bread fall on the ground.

Syria: The *Didascalia Apostolorum*

While this early third-century church order does not offer much of a description of the sequence and contents of the eucharistic celebration, what it does provide is a particularly clear description as to how the author expected the worshipping assembly to be ordered in that part of the world. It instructs the bishops thus:

> And in your congregations in the holy churches hold your assemblies with all decent order, and appoint the places for the brethren with care and gravity. For the presbyters a place in the easternmost part of the house should be assigned, and let the bishop's throne be placed in their midst, and let the presbyters sit with him.
>
> And again, let the lay men sit in another part of the house towards the east. For thus it should be, that in the most easterly part of the house the presbyters sit with the bishops, next the lay men, and then the women; so that when you stand up to pray, the leaders may stand first, and after them the lay men, and then the women too. For it is requisite that you pray facing the east, aware that it is written, 'Give glory to God, who rides upon the heavens of heavens towards the east' [Ps. 68.34].[10]

---

9 See further Phillips, *The Ritual Kiss in Early Christian Worship*, pp. 19–21. The exchange of a kiss at the conclusion of prayer is also mentioned in *Apostolic Tradition* 18: see Bradshaw, Johnson and Phillips, *The Apostolic Tradition*, pp. 99–100.
10 *Didascalia Apostolorum* 2.57; ET from Michael Vasey and Sebastian Brock, *The Liturgical Portions of the Didascalia* (Nottingham, 1982), pp. 15–16.

The instructions then go on to direct that the young are to sit separately, as are the elderly; children are to stand on one side or be close to their parents; young girls should sit separately, or if there is no room, should stand up behind the women; young women who are married and have children should stand separately, and elderly women and widows should sit separately. It is the duty of the deacons to ensure that people go to their proper place and behave appropriately. The deacons are also to direct any visitors from other congregations to sit with the appropriate group within the assembly, including seating presbyters with the resident presbyters and a bishop with the resident bishop.

It is impossible to be sure how far these detailed arrangements reflect actual liturgical practice in that part of the world and how far they existed only as ideals in the compiler's mind. Certainly the separation of men and women in the assembly could have been the result of the influence of the surrounding culture. Although there is no evidence of gender segregation in the Jewish synagogue in this early period, it was normal at public events such as the theatre and the circus in the Graeco-Roman world. Moreover, where respectable women were present at banquets in antiquity, they would also usually have been seated separately from the men, and such segregation may even have persisted at the earliest Christian eucharistic meals and developed from there into the practice that we find here.[11]

While the section of the text quoted above does not give any indication whether the gathering was for a service of the word or for the celebration of the Eucharist, its instructions concerning the deacons make it clear that the Eucharist is in mind: 'let one always stand by the offerings of the Eucharist; and let another stand outside the door and observe those who enter. But afterwards, when you offer the oblation, let them serve together in the church.' A little later it goes on to give a particularly interesting directive as to what the resident bishop should ask an episcopal visitor to do: he should invite him to give a homily, 'and when you offer the oblation, let him speak the words; but if he is wise and gives the honour to you, and is unwilling to offer, at least let him speak the words over the cup'.[12] Earlier scholars were generally somewhat puzzled by this instruction. As they presumed that the eucharistic prayer in use was a continuous whole, and believed that it included the institution narrative, they were forced to conclude that it

---

11 See Teresa Berger, *Women's Ways of Worship* (Collegeville, 1999), pp. 34–6 and 54–6.
12 *Didascalia* 2.58; ET from Vasey and Brock, *The Liturgical Portions of the Didascalia*, p. 16.

must have meant that the visiting bishop was simply to recite Jesus' words relating to the cup. But if separate prayer units over bread and cup were still in use, the direction becomes very much clearer: the visitor was to recite the prayer over the cup and the resident bishop the prayer over the bread.[13] Does this particular distribution of roles also imply that the cup prayer came first, before the bread prayer, or not?

A later section of the church order confirms that this was a gathering for both word and sacrament and that it took place on a Sunday, but gives no indication as to the time of day that it occurred:

> Do not consider your worldly affairs more important than the word of God; but on the Lord's day leave everything and dash eagerly to your church, for it is your glory. Otherwise, what excuse before God have those who do not assemble on the Lord's day to hear the word of life and to be nourished with the divine food which abides for ever?[14]

Nevertheless, this exhortation goes on to imply that not all Christians were choosing to put attendance at Sunday worship before attendance at theatrical performances.

Some light is shed on the compiler's theology of eucharistic consecration elsewhere in the document. It directs that, in contrast to Old Testament law that regarded touching corpses as defiling and so requiring ritual ablution, Christians are to

> gather together actually in the cemeteries, and read the holy Scriptures, and without any such observances perform your ministry and your supplication to God; and offer an acceptable Eucharist, the likeness of the body of Christ,[15] both in your congregation and in your cemeteries and on the departures of those who are fallen asleep; – pure bread that is made with fire, and sanctified by means of invocations; and without doubting you should pray and offer for those who have fallen asleep.[16]

---

13 Thus Marcel Metzger, 'The *Didascalia* and *Constitutiones Apostolorum*', in *The Eucharist of the Early Christians* (New York, 1978), p. 202; Mazza, *The Origins of the Eucharistic Prayer*, p. 59.

14 *Didascalia* 2.59; ET from Vasey and Brock, *The Liturgical Portions of the Didascalia*, pp. 17–18.

15 Other mss have 'likeness of the body, the kingdom of Christ'.

16 *Didascalia* 6.22; ET from Vasey and Brock, *The Liturgical Portions of the Didascalia*, p. 33.

At an earlier point it had spoken of the Eucharist being 'accepted and sanctified through the Holy Spirit',[17] and so taking these two passages together suggests that the sanctification of bread and cup was understood to take place as a result of the invocation of the Holy Spirit. The first quotation also discloses that the Eucharist might be celebrated in cemeteries at funerals and also probably on the anniversary of death. It appears to be an attempt to provide a Christian substitute for the widespread pagan custom of the *refrigerium* ('refreshment'), a graveside funeral feast supposedly shared with the departed, which was opposed by Christians both because of the riotous behaviour that tended to arise from such occasions and because of the implications it had regarding the state of the departed.[18]

We can also see signs in this church order of an emerging sacerdotal understanding of the ordained ministry. While the author continues to call the whole Church a priesthood (quoting 1 Peter 2.9) and instructs the people to offer up prayers, petitions and thanksgivings in place of the former sacrifices, this is to be done through the bishops: 'For they are your high priests, whereas the priests and levites of today are the presbyters and deacons, and the orphans and widows; but the levitical high priest is the bishop.'[19] The context, together with inclusion of the orphans and widows along with the other ministers, indicates that this sacerdotal imagery is being used primarily to justify the right of all these classes of people to receive from the congregation 'offerings and tithes and first fruits' for their financial support rather than to demarcate a ministerial priesthood acting on behalf of the laity; but taken in conjunction with the statement that such offerings are to be made 'through the bishops' and with the instruction to the bishops concerning the Eucharist cited earlier, 'when *you* offer the oblation', it is clear that such an idea is in the process of emerging.

Alexandria: Clement and Origen

Most historians of the Eucharist pass over in silence or with the briefest of references the writings of Clement of Alexandria (*c.* 160–215 CE) and

17 *Didascalia* 6.21; ET from Vasey and Brock, *The Liturgical Portions of the Didascalia*, p. 32.
18 Tertullian claimed he could see no difference between the *refrigerium* and a feast of Jupiter, and criticized those who took part for presenting the offerings to themselves rather than the departed and for returning home drunk (*Apol.* 13.7; *De test. animae* 4).
19 *Didascalia* 2.26; ET from Vasey and Brock, *The Liturgical Portions of the Didascalia*, p. 11.

Origen (*c.* 185–*c.* 251 CE), and to a considerable extent rightly so. Although these two theologians do appear to make many passing allusions in their works to ideas that could be connected with the Eucharist, the obscure nature of their discourse makes it very difficult to know exactly what they might have meant in most cases. On the other hand, the few scholars who have plunged into the wealth of allegory and philosophical speculation in these Alexandrian authors have sometimes seen eucharistic allusions in places where others might hesitate to suggest them.[20] In any case, it is questionable how far the ideas put forward by these two members of a rarified elite among Alexandrian Christians can be thought to be at all representative of what ordinary members of the Church in that part of the world were taught or believed about eucharistic theology. There is also the same problem encountered in the sources I have examined earlier, of knowing whether many of the allusions to liturgical practices are to the Eucharist or to an independent service of the word.

Nevertheless, it is perhaps possible to extract from this morass a few indications of what eucharistic practice might have included. Clement gives some information on the posture adopted for prayer in general (raising head and hands towards heaven, and facing east: *Strom.* 7.7), which we may reasonably presume also applied to prayer at the Eucharist, and he also refers to the exchange of the kiss in liturgical assemblies, criticizing those who perform the action noisily but lack the love that should accompany it (*Paed.* 3.11). There is also a somewhat obscure allusion to some who, when distributing the Eucharist, apparently allow believers to take a portion of it for themselves – presumably rather than having it handed to them (*Strom.* 1.1). Clement opposes the use by some of the name *agape* for their over-indulgent feasts, thereby dishonouring the true *agape*, 'for the supper takes place because of love (*agape*), but the supper is not love (*agape*).' The diet should instead be light and digestible (*Paed.* 2.1). While scholars have generally adhered to the common assumption that the *agape* was something distinct from the Eucharist, it should be noted that there is nothing in the text itself that points to that conclusion, and no mention anywhere in Clement's writing of the two as being separate.

Origen has a little more to say. He too mentions the exchange of the kiss at the conclusion of prayer (*Comm. in Rom.* 10.33), he indicates that the word 'Eucharist' was used to designate the consecrated bread (*Contra Celsum* 8.57), and he alludes in passing to the care believers take

---

20 See, for example, André Méhat, 'Clement of Alexandria', in *The Eucharist of the Early Christians*, pp. 99–131.

in ensuring that no fragment of that bread falls from their hands on to the ground when they receive it (*Hom. in Exod.* 13.3). We have already referred to a similar statement in Tertullian in connection with wine and bread (*De cor.* 3), and an admonition to exercise caution in relation to the bread occurs in *Apostolic Tradition* 37 too, though there apparently in connection with bread being kept in the home for communion.[21] In addition, Origen speaks about eucharistic consecration: 'we, giving thanks to the Creator of all, also eat the bread that is presented with thanksgiving and prayer over what is given; and it becomes through prayer a holy body and sanctifies those who partake of it with pure intention' (*Contra Celsum* 8.33). Similarly, he elsewhere echoes 1 Timothy 4.5 when he speaks of the eucharistic bread being sanctified by the word of God and prayer (*Comm. in Matt.* 11.14), but offers no more detailed explanation of the nature of the prayer that effects the sanctification.

It should also be noted that he consistently described bishops as priests (see, e.g., *De or.* 28), but not 'high priests', as in the *Didascalia*, and he also speaks of presbyters as exercising an inferior form of priesthood (*Hom. in Exod.* 11.6; *Hom. in Lev.* 6.6). This latter concept was possibly inspired by a phrase in 2 Kings 23.4 ('the priests of the second order'), and is one which recurs in later writings, including the later Roman ordination prayer for a presbyter. Although such language would seem to imply that Origen viewed the ordained ministry as therefore offering the eucharistic sacrifice on behalf of the people, rather than the people as a whole making the offering, he is not explicit about this.

North Africa: Cyprian

Whatever may have been the situation in north Africa in Tertullian's time, it appears that by the middle of the third century the Eucharist was certainly being celebrated in the morning. In the year 253 Cyprian wrote a letter to a certain Caecilius, Bishop of Biltha, contending strongly against the use of water alone in the cup, to which I have referred to in an earlier chapter,[22] and in the course of this lengthy treatise, he also reveals other aspects of contemporary eucharistic practice and theology. One of the major planks of his argument for the use of wine mixed with water was that Christians must follow in their celebration exactly what Christ did at the Last Supper. However, he had then to deal with the difficulty that Christ's Supper took place in the evening, but

---

21 See Bradshaw, Johnson and Phillips, *Apostolic Tradition*, p. 182.
22 See above, pp. 54–5.

the custom with which he was apparently familiar was of a morning celebration. He did so by claiming that Christ's action signified the end of the old age, whereas Christians celebrate the dawn of the new:

> But still it was not in the morning, but after supper that the Lord offered the mixed cup. Ought we therefore to celebrate the Lord's (sacrifice?) after supper, that we may thus offer the mixed cup when attending the Lord's (sacrifice?)? It was fitting for Christ to offer about the evening of the day, so that the very hour of sacrifice might show the setting and evening of the world, as it is written in Exodus, 'And all the people of the synagogue of the children of Israel shall kill it in the evening'; and again in the Psalms, 'the lifting up of my hands (as) an evening sacrifice'. But we celebrate the resurrection of the Lord in the morning. (*Ep.* 63.16.2–4)

On the other hand, Andrew McGowan argues that the transition from evening to morning celebration was in fact only just taking place in other parts of the local province and so was still the subject of some debate. For Cyprian had just said in his letter: 'Does any one perhaps flatter himself with the thought that even if in the morning water alone is seen to be offered, yet when we come to supper, we offer the mixed cup? But when we dine, we cannot call the people together to our banquet so that we may celebrate the truth of the sacrament with all the brotherhood present' (*Ep.* 63.16.1). McGowan understands this to mean that Cyprian's opponents are saying that while they drink water at their morning assembly, they do use the mixed cup of wine at their evening supper, to which Cyprian responds that the evening gathering is unsuitable because it is not possible to assemble the whole Christian community in one place for a supper.[23]

From this, McGowan concludes that while Cyprian's own church in Carthage seems to have moved decisively to morning eucharistic celebrations some considerable time earlier because of the problem of catering for very large numbers, other congregations in smaller towns around were still continuing to have something quite similar to what we appear to encounter in Tertullian some fifty years before, both an evening supper and a morning distribution of communion on another day. The sole difference seems to be that the people addressed here by Cyprian are distributing only water and not wine with the bread at these morning assemblies, which may by now have become full eucharistic

---

23 'Rethinking Agape and Eucharist in Early North African Christianity'.

celebrations, even though the evening suppers also continued alongside them. Their justification – or rationalization – for this particular mixed practice is also revealed by Cyprian in the letter: they appear to be afraid that the smell of wine on their breath in the morning might give them away as being Christians during the persecution that the Church was currently undergoing. Cyprian's response was characteristically robust: 'How can we shed our blood for Christ, who blush to drink the blood of Christ?' (*Ep.* 63.15).

What we also learn from this substantial letter about the Eucharist is that Cyprian understood there to be a very close connection between the eucharistic offering made by the Church and Christ's sacrificial death on the cross, developing this idea much further than any of his predecessors whose writings have survived. I suggested earlier[24] that Cyprian was influenced by the New Testament narratives of the Last Supper more than others before him because of the status as Scripture that these writings were now acquiring, and so this factor supplies one reason for such a theological development. But the evolution in thought may well be also not unrelated to the experience of persecution and the constant threat of a possible imminent martyr's death similar to that of Jesus which believers were facing at the time. Like Justin and Irenaeus before him, Cyprian asserts that what is offered is the bread and cup (*Ep.* 63.2, 9, and *passim*), and he is explicit that this is done in remembrance of Christ, *in commemorationem eius* (*Ep.* 63.2 and 14), 'in remembrance of the Lord and of his passion' (*Ep.* 63.17). But he goes further than this, and describes the act as being 'the sacrament of our Lord's passion and of our redemption' (*Ep.* 63.14) and even says that 'we make mention of his passion in all sacrifices, for the Lord's passion is the sacrifice that we offer' (*Ep.* 63.17).

This language arose out of the same principle of the necessity of imitating Christ that Cyprian had used to argue against the use of water alone in the Eucharist: 'Hence it appears that the blood of Christ is not offered if wine is absent from the cup, nor the Lord's sacrifice celebrated with a legitimate consecration unless our oblation and sacrifice correspond to the passion' (*Ep.* 63.9). In the Eucharist the Church must not only imitate Christ's action at the Supper but also his sacrifice of himself on the cross:

> For if Jesus Christ, our Lord and God, is himself the high priest of God the Father and first offered himself as a sacrifice to the Father, and commanded this to be done in his remembrance, then that

---

24 See above, pp. 17–18.

priest truly functions in the place of Christ who imitates what Christ did and then offers a true and full sacrifice in the church to God the Father, if he thus proceeds to offer according to what he sees Christ himself to have offered. (*Ep.* 63.14)

But what exactly does this mean? Scholars have been divided. Some would interpret Cyprian as saying that in the Eucharist the priest offers the same sacrifice that Christ offered on the cross, that is, he 'offers Christ'. While this is certainly the first place where the priest is said to function 'in the place of Christ' (*vice Christi*), other scholars do not think that the image should be taken quite so literally, that it means something like: 'just as Christ offered himself as a sacrifice, so too does the priest offer the Church's sacrifice in memory of him'.[25] If that is so, then Cyprian's remarks that 'the Lord's passion is the sacrifice which we offer' and 'the blood of Christ . . . is offered' should be understood in the light of that.

What does stand out from this letter is that the eucharistic offering is now thought of as being made *by* the ordained ministers *for* the people rather than as being the action of the priestly people as whole. The bishop is the one whom Cyprian designates here and elsewhere as *sacerdos*, 'priest', reserving *summus sacerdos*, 'high-priest', for Christ alone (*Ep.* 63.14), though he also describes presbyters as participating in the episcopal *sacerdotium* (see, e.g., *Ep.* 1.1; 61.3). Thus when he talks about 'us' being 'priests of God and of Christ' (*Ep.* 63.18), and of it pertaining to 'the office of our priesthood' to mix and offer the cup of the Lord (*Ep.* 63.19), it is evident that it is his episcopal colleagues to whom he is referring and not to Christians in general (see *Ep.* 63.18). This shift in ecclesiology and eucharistic theology was perhaps a more or less inevitable development once sacerdotal language had begun to be adopted for the ordained ministry, but it was doubtless also encouraged by the contemporary social situation of the city churches in north Africa, which required a strong and structured leadership rather than a loose association of believers because congregations were apparently growing much larger in size, acquiring substantial property and income, and even paying salaries to their clergy. Thus, although later liturgical texts might continue to carry the more ancient image of the common priesthood in which all Christians participated, in theological discourse and liturgical practice bishops and presbyters would cease to be seen as the presiders within a priestly people, and become instead a priesthood

---

25 See further John D. Laurance, *Priest as Type of Christ: The Leader of the Eucharist in Salvation History According to Cyprian of Carthage* (New York, 1984).

acting on behalf of 'the laity' – a term that had already been used in this sense as early as *1 Clem.* 40.5. It is true that in another of Cyprian's works, on the Lord's Prayer, he does speak of 'when we come together with our brothers and celebrate the divine sacrifices with God's priest' (*De dom. or.* 4), but he does not use the term 'offer' here to refer to the action of the people and appears to find it necessary to include specific mention of the priest, which does seem to concur with the eucharistic theology of *Ep.* 63.

Just as the possibility of impending martyrdom for believers may have played a part in shaping Cyprian's eucharistic theology, so too the threats posed by apostasy and schism during his episcopate made him equally conscious of the ecclesiological dimension of the Eucharist. He believed that it was only within the one true Church that the Eucharist could be genuinely celebrated, only within the body of Christ that believers could be truly united with their Lord. Thus he says: 'Christ is the bread of those who are in union with his body' (*De dom. or.* 18). Similarly, commenting on Exodus 12.46 ('In one house shall it be eaten; you shall not carry forth any of the flesh outside the home'), he says: 'The flesh of Christ and the holy (*sanctum*) of the Lord cannot be carried abroad, nor is there any other home for believers but the one church' (*De unit. eccl.* 8).

Other writings of Cyprian furnish us with some more details of eucharistic practice. He is the first to tell us that the invitation, 'Lift up your hearts', with its response 'We lift them up to the Lord', was regularly used at the beginning of the eucharistic prayer (*De dom. or.* 31). He also speaks of Christians receiving 'the Eucharist daily as the food of salvation' (ibid., 18) and of drinking 'the cup of Christ's blood daily' so that they may be able to shed their blood for Christ (*Ep.* 58.1), but it is not clear that this must necessarily denote that there was commonly a daily celebration of the Eucharist, at least during periods of persecution if not more generally. It is possible that it could simply mean that Christians continued to take the consecrated elements home from the Sunday Eucharist for daily consumption. The more usual practice seems to have been for bread alone to be reserved in this way, apparently because of the difficulty of preserving wine. Cyprian himself, as a warning against unworthy reception of communion, tells the story of a woman who tried with impure hands to open the container (*arcam*) in which she was keeping the body of Christ, but fire flared up from it and prevented her touching it (*De lapsis* 26). Nevertheless, it is conceivable that attempts were being made to reserve wine as well during the time of persecution precisely because of the intimate connection that was seen between the blood of Christ and the blood that the believer might be called upon to

shed. A passage in the *Apostolic Tradition* (38A) may refer to this
practice, though its meaning is not entirely clear.[26] Both Cyprian and
this church order certainly understood the eucharistic elements as
having apotropaic powers to protect those who receive it, and this would
have supplied a strong motivation for its daily reception: 'as the
Eucharist exists for this purpose, that it can be a safeguard for those
receiving it, let us arm those whom we wish to be safe against the adver-
sary with the protection of the Lord's abundance' (Cyprian, *Ep*. 57.2);
'Let every faithful person try to receive the Eucharist before he tastes
anything, for if he receives in faith, even if someone may give him something deadly after this, it will not overpower him' (*Apostolic Tradition* 36,
Greek fragment).

On the other hand, *Ep*. 57.3 does seem more naturally to imply the
existence of a daily Eucharist: 'it is the great honour and glory of our
episcopate to have granted peace to martyrs, so that we, as priests who
daily celebrate the sacrifices of God, may prepare offerings and victims
for God' – the 'offerings and victims' here being actually Christians who
are prepared to die as martyrs. While it is just possible that the daily celebration of 'the sacrifices of God' could refer to the mention of these
individuals in the daily prayers and not necessarily in a daily Eucharist,
that would not be in line with Cyprian's normal use of the term. Similarly, the reference in *Ep*. 5 to 'the presbyters who offer in the presence of
the confessors' in prison does seem to indicate not only that eucharistic
celebrations could take place in situations other than in the midst of the
local congregation, and probably on days other than Sunday, but also
that presbyters as well as bishops might occasionally preside at them, at
least during periods of persecution. The latter is confirmed by other
letters (e.g., *Ep*. 15.1; 17.2), where Cyprian criticizes those presbyters
who dare 'to offer' on behalf of the lapsed and to give them communion
before they have done penance and been reconciled.

Regardless of whether or not the Eucharist was celebrated on a daily
basis, there is some evidence pointing to celebrations on the anniversaries of the deaths of martyrs and confessors in Cyprian's church.
He says of certain individuals who have suffered death in this way:
'we always offer sacrifices for them, as you remember, as often as we
celebrate the passions and days of the martyrs in the annual commemoration' (*Ep*. 39.3). And he writes to his clergy and instructs them to
take note of the date of the death of those who died in prison after
confessing the faith, 'so that we may be able to celebrate their commemoration among the memorials of the martyrs' and he tells them that for

---

26 See Bradshaw, Johnson and Phillips, *The Apostolic Tradition*, pp. 184–5.

those whose dates he already knows, 'there are celebrated here by us oblations and sacrifices for their commemorations, which, with the Lord's protection, we shall soon celebrate with you' (*Ep.* 12.2). There is also a reference to the Eucharist being offered for the repose of deceased persons in *Ep.* 1.2. Whether this took place within the regular Sunday liturgy or at a special weekday celebration is not specified, but it is revealed that on such occasions the deceased would normally have their names mentioned 'at God's altar in the prayer of the priests'.

Finally, in order to complete the account of the knowledge that we gain about the Eucharist from Cyprian's correspondence, we should add that among the collected letters is one from Firmilian, Bishop of Caesarea in Cappadocia, to Cyprian that tells of a self-proclaimed prophetess around the year 230 who, according to the author, had deceived many and 'pretended to sanctify bread and to make the Eucharist with a passable invocation, and she offered sacrifice to the Lord [not] without the sacrament of customary pronouncement' (*Ep.* 75.10). Although there is no manuscript support for the insertion of the word 'not', it is often added on the grounds that the sense requires it.

At the turn of the century

Cyprian is the last major witness to eucharistic theology and practice in the third century. We know nothing of further developments in the second half of the century, and indeed it will be another hundred years after Cyprian before our next major witness emerges. Hence we must beware of making generalizations about the century as a whole on such a limited range of evidence, from so few centres of Christianity, and from such a restricted time-frame. Nevertheless, on the basis of the material we have surveyed, there are indications that the association of the Eucharist with a substantial meal was declining, and at least in some places had disappeared altogether by the middle of the century if not sooner. There are also signs of a trend to locate the eucharistic celebration in the morning rather than the evening, probably in connection with a service of the word, though that is by no means as clearly attested as one might have thought or wished. In addition, our Syrian source, the *Didascalia*, indicates the existence of additional eucharistic celebrations in cemeteries, very likely on days other than Sunday, and our African witnesses testify to the emergence of celebrations on the anniversaries of martyrs, if not more frequently still. The widespread application of sacerdotal language to the bishop (and by association to other ordained ministers) heralds a growing shift towards regarding the eucharistic president, rather than the priestly people, as the principal agent in the offering of the eucharistic sacrifice; and Cyprian's close linkage of that offering with the death of Christ marks a turning point in eucharistic thinking that is destined to have a profound effect upon later doctrine.

Beyond that, however, we know scarcely any more about the details of eucharistic practice, the shape of the rite, or how people understood it at this period. We could of course do what some earlier historians did and create a single composite picture by putting together all the fragments of information we have from the time of Justin Martyr down to Cyprian and then supplementing that with material known only from the middle of the fourth century onwards, on the assumption that it must have remained constant for a hundred years or more. But that would not be methodologically sound, and so we must rest content with the partial glimpses into third-century eucharistic practices and theologies that our few extant sources afford us.

Chapter 7

The Evolution of Eucharistic Prayers

Scholarly opinion has been all but unanimous in seeing the origin of Christian eucharistic prayers as lying in the Jewish grace after meals, the *Birkat ha-mazon*, or an earlier version of it. This supposition is perhaps not surprising. In looking for a plausible Jewish ancestry for the quite substantial and – at least ostensibly – unitary compositions in use as eucharistic prayers from the late fourth century onwards, it was natural that the choice should fall on the longer grace after meals, presumed to have been said over the cup in Christian circles, rather than the brief formula it was assumed would have been used over bread at the beginning of the meal.

However, this view needs to be challenged. First, it faces the difficulty of explaining how a prayer originally said at the end of a meal could come to be used as a prayer of thanksgiving over both bread and cup at the outset before they were consumed. The suggestion that the sacramental elements of bread and wine were at an early stage separated from the rest of the meal and transferred to the end, after this final prayer, offers a convenient solution to the problem, but lacks any actual evidence to support it. Second, specific resemblances between the *Birkat ha-mazon* and later Christian eucharistic prayers are extremely limited. The Christian prayers often do not refer to any of the particular themes found in the former, and so the most that can be said is that both offer praise for what God is believed to have done and then make petition for eschatological fulfilment in one form or another. If there is any connection, therefore, it is very vague and indirect.

Developments of *Didache* 9—10

The three sets of prayers from fourth-century sources in Table 3 obviously have some connection with the material in *Didache* 9—10. But what precisely is their relationship? The prayers from *Apostolic*

Constitutions Book 7 are part of a reworking of the whole of the *Didache* in that book, and the connection in this case is literary. The compiler of the *Apostolic Constitutions* had before him the text of the *Didache* and adapted it in the light of his own situation.[1] We may note that several significant changes have been made to the material from *Didache* 9—10 here. The order has been changed to the more 'normal' sequence, so that what had been the thanksgiving over the bread comes first, followed by its linked petition and then by what had been the thanksgiving over the cup, all three units now part of one continuous prayer. The distribution then follows, and the prayer in *Didache* 10, the grace after eating, has become a lengthy post-communion prayer. The theology expressed in the text also shows a considerable advance on the primitive ideas in the *Didache*. In what is now the first unit the Christological anamnesis has been filled out, so that it recalls the incarnation, passion, resurrection, seating in glory and hope for the *eschaton*; and in the final unit mention of the vine of David has disappeared and replaced by a reference to the 'precious blood of Jesus Christ poured out for us'. To this has been added mention of 'his precious body' with an explicit eucharistic reference: 'of which we celebrate this antitype'.

However, does it represent actual liturgical practice in the fourth century, as Marcel Metzger concluded?[2] The prayers are so different in character from the eucharistic rite which occurs in Book 8 of the *Apostolic Constitutions* and is derived from the *Apostolic Tradition* that it is hard to believe that both types could have been current alongside one another in the same liturgical community. That seems to leave just two alternative possibilities: that it reflects an archaic pattern no longer in use, which has to some extent been modified by the redactor of the *Apostolic Constitutions*, or that it is a completely artificial construction attempting to revise the text of the *Didache* but not representative of real eucharistic worship anywhere. It is difficult to choose between the two. For help in that, we need to turn to the other texts in the table.

In the case of the Sacramentary of Sarapion, what is reproduced here is just the middle section of the complete eucharistic prayer. The petitionary prayer in the heart of it appears to be based on that in the *Didache*, but what precedes and follows it are elements of the institution

---

1 Greek text in Marcel Metzger (ed.), *Les Constitutions apostoliques*, 3 vols (Paris, 1985–7). For the origin of the *Apostolic Constitutions* in general, see Bradshaw, *The Search for the Origins of Christian Worship*, pp. 84–6.

2 'Les deux prières eucharistiques des Constitutions apostoliques', *RSR* (1971), pp. 52–77. He thought that it might still have been used at less important and more modest celebrations while the more developed prayer in Book 8 was used on other occasions (p. 77).

Table 3: Developments of Didache 9—10

Apostolic Constitutions 7.25–6	Sarapion, Prayer 1	De Virginitate 12–13
Always be thankful, as faithful and honest servants, and concerning the eucharist saying thus:		*And when you sit down at table and come to break the bread, having signed yourself three times, say thus, giving thanks:*
We give thanks to you, our Father, for that life which you have made known to us through Jesus your child, through whom you made all things and care for the whole world; whom you sent to become human for our salvation; whom you permitted to suffer and to die; whom you raised up, and were pleased to glorify and set down on your right hand; by whom you promised us the resurrection of the dead.	To you we offered this bread, the likeness of the body of the only-begotten. This bread is the likeness of the holy body, because the Lord Jesus Christ, in the night when he was betrayed, took bread and broke (it) and gave (it) to his disciples, saying, 'Take and eat; this is my body which is broken for you for forgiveness of sins.' Therefore we also offered the bread making the likeness of the death, and we beseech through this sacrifice, be reconciled to us all and be merciful, God of truth.	We give thanks to you, our Father, for your holy resurrection. For through your servant Jesus Christ you have made it known to us.
Do you, almighty Lord, everlasting God, as this was scattered, and having been gathered together became one bread, so gather together your church from the ends of the earth into your kingdom.	And as this bread was scattered upon the mountains and having been gathered together became into one, so gather together your holy church out of every people and every land and every city and street and house, and make one living catholic church.	And as this bread which (is) on this table was scattered and being gathered together became one, so may your church be gathered together from the ends of the earth into your kingdom; for yours is the power and the glory, to the ages of ages. Amen.
We also give thanks, our Father, for the precious blood of Jesus Christ poured out for us and his precious body, of which we celebrate this antitype, as he commanded us, 'to proclaim his death'. For through him glory (be) to you for evermore. Amen.	And we also offered the cup, the likeness of the blood, because the Lord Jesus Christ, having taken a cup after the supper, said to his disciples, 'Take, drink; this is the new covenant, which is my blood poured out for you for forgiveness of sins.' Therefore we also offered the cup, presenting the likeness of blood.	

Table 3: continued

Apostolic Constitutions 7.25–6	Sarapion, Prayer 1	De Virginitate 12–13
Let none of the uninitiated eat of these things, but only those baptized in the death of the Lord . . . After the participation, give thanks thus:		*After the service of the ninth (hour), eat your food, having given thanks to God over your table thus:*
We give thanks to you, the God and Father of Jesus our Saviour, for your holy name, which you have enshrined in us; and for the knowledge and faith and love and immortality which you have given us through Jesus your child. You, Almighty Lord, the God of the universe, who created the world and everything in it through him, have planted a law in our souls, and prepared in advance things for the participation of humans. God of our holy and blameless fathers, Abraham and Isaac and Jacob, your faithful servants, mighty God, faithful and true and without deceit in promises, who sent on earth Jesus your Christ to live with humans as human, being God the Word and human, to take away error by the roots, even now, through him, remember this your holy church, which you have purchased with the precious blood of your Christ, and deliver it from all evil and perfect it in your love and your truth, and gather us all together into your kingdom which you have prepared for it. Maranatha. Hosanna to the Son of David. Blessed (be) the one coming in (the) name of (the) Lord, God (the) Lord, manifested to us in flesh. If anyone (is) holy, let him come near; but if anyone is not, let him become (so) by repentance.		Blessed be God, who has nourished me from my youth, who gives food to all flesh. Fill my heart with joy and gladness that always having a sufficiency in all things, we may abound to every good work in Christ Jesus our Lord, with whom to you (is) glory, honour, power, with the Holy Spirit to the ages of ages. Amen.
Allow also your presbyters to give thanks.		

narrative and not *Didache* thanksgiving material, though they occur in the same order as in *Apostolic Constitutions* 7, that is, the material relating to the bread first and that to the cup after the petitionary unit. I noted above in Chapter 1 the peculiar form of the institution narrative in this prayer, and observed then that several scholars had proposed that behind it actually lay a much older pattern of eucharistic rite.[3] Klaus Gamber thought that the original form of the prayer had consisted merely of a series of thanksgivings followed by the petitionary unit of *Didache* 9.4 and had been a prayer over the bread alone;[4] Edward Kilmartin believed that the separation of the words concerning the bread and the cup by the quotation of *Didache* 9.4 in the prayer as it now stands 'probably reflects a former practice in Egypt of introducing the meal between the Eucharistic rites';[5] and Louis Bouyer thought that the structure: bread words/*Didache* 9.4/cup words, 'leads one to think that it resulted from remodeling found in the 7th book of the *Apostolic Constitutions*'.[6] But it is Enrico Mazza who has come closer to the truth in identifying both this section of Sarapion's eucharistic prayer and also the material in *Apostolic Constitutions* 7 (however artificial the latter may be in its present form) as deriving from a common source representative of what he describes – somewhat over-confidently – as 'the ancient and paleoanaphoric structure of the Eucharistic celebration'.[7] This conclusion has been broadly endorsed by Maxwell Johnson.[8]

More light may be shed on the history by the third source, part of the rule for virgins that was formerly believed to have been the work of Athanasius but now generally acknowledged to be of Cappadocian origin and dating from the second half of the fourth century.[9] The order of the material from this document has been rearranged in my table because, although what I have shown as the final prayer comes first in the text and is probably meant to be said before the meal, a later direction contradicts this and states that it is to be said after the meal. The texts are intended to provide forms of grace for use at the community's

---

3 See above, p. 21.

4 'Die Serapion-Anaphora ihrem ältesten Bestand nach untersucht', *L'Orient syrien* 16 (1967), pp. 23–42, here at pp. 40–1.

5 'Sacrificium Laudis: Content and Function of Early Eucharistic Prayers', *TS* 35 (1974), pp. 268–87, here at p. 284.

6 *Eucharist*, p. 208.

7 *The Origins of the Eucharistic Prayer*, p. 228.

8 *The Prayers of Sarapion of Thmuis: A Literary, Liturgical, and Theological Analysis* (Rome, 1995), p. 226.

9 Greek text in E. F. von der Goltz (ed.), *De virginitate. Eine echte Schrift des Athanasius* (Leipzig, 1905), pp. 46–7.

normal daily mealtime rather than a eucharistic rite, but appear to have some relation to the material in the *Didache*. The parallel to *Didache* 9.4 is obvious in the petitionary unit and something like 9.3 seems to lie behind the initial thanksgiving, but the concluding prayer possibly derives from another source altogether, but one that still retains a strongly Jewish flavour. The absence of a parallel for the cup-blessing of *Didache* 9.2 is no doubt to be accounted for by the absence of wine from the community's daily meal. All this suggests that we are dealing with the product of a living tradition here that shared features in common with the *Didache* material rather than a literary adaptation of that particular text.

Taken together, these three texts seem to point to the conclusion that the sort of prayers found in *Didache* 9—10 continued to be used at least within certain segments of early Christianity for a considerable number of years, although rearranged in the course of time so that the prayer over the bread came before that over the cup. How long they remained in use for eucharistic worship and how widely they were disseminated is impossible to say in the absence of further evidence. Cyprian clearly knows the metaphor of the bread scattered and brought together,[10] but whether he was familiar with more of this prayer tradition or whether that was merely a common eucharistic image circulating independently we cannot determine. It seems unlikely, however, that the prayers would have survived in use into the fourth century, except as table prayers for daily meals. Thus this particular Jewish trajectory eventually ran into the ground, and so we must look elsewhere for the roots of later eucharistic prayers.

The persistence of multiple prayer units

Because most later eucharistic prayers have at least the initial appearance of unitary compositions running seamlessly from opening salutation to final doxology, scholars have tended to assume that this was the case from very early times and have generally looked for a unitary composition as the ancestor of these later forms. They have been encouraged in this line of enquiry by the eucharistic prayer in the so-called *Apostolic Tradition* of Hippolytus, which also has a similar unitary appearance and which it has commonly been assumed represented mainstream liturgical practice of the early third century, if not long before then.

---

10 *Ep.* 63.13: 'just as many grains, collected and ground and mixed together into one, make one bread, so in Christ, who is the heavenly bread, we may know that there is one body, with which our number is joined and united.'

However, this text presents something of a red herring in the search for the roots of eucharistic prayers. Not only does its present form seem to belong to the fourth century rather than the third,[11] but even its older source may not have been as typical of early eucharistic practice as many have supposed.

We have seen that longer Jewish prayers were usually made up of a combination of quite short units, and the Christian material in *Didache* 9—10 continues to reflect that construction. The development of this material which I have examined above shows how these units could continue to be moved around and rearranged to form different patterns as well as modified in wording even after their initial juxtaposition. When we look below more closely at what are often thought to be some very early eucharistic prayers, the Anaphora of Addai and Mari and the Strasbourg Papyrus, we shall see evidence that they too were constructed in a similar fashion, by the conjunction of discrete prayer units. This suggests that the Jewish practice of assembling prayers by joining together the building-blocks of individual prayer units may have survived and been at least as common in early Christianity as the creation of a through-composed eucharistic text. I have already noted earlier the suggestion by Enrico Mazza that, contrary to the usual opinion, Justin Martyr may have been familiar with separate prayer units over bread and cup rather than a single prayer over both because of his use of the plural, when he says that the president 'sends up prayer*s* and thanksgiving*s* to the best of his ability' (*I Apol.* 67.5); and also Mazza's further suggestion that the persistence of separate prayers would explain the otherwise enigmatic direction in the third-century Syrian *Didascalia Apostolorum* that if a visiting bishop does not wish to accept the invitation to preside over the whole eucharistic offering, he should at least 'say the words over the cup'.[12] If this was indeed the pattern that much eucharistic praying once took, it means that the process of adding further components – including the Sanctus and institution narrative – that we encounter from the fourth century onwards does not represent an alien intrusion into what were formerly unitary creations, but was simply continuing a tradition of combining smaller units together that was at the heart of many ancient compositions

Sadly, however, we cannot follow Mazza in his overall hypothesis concerning the development of eucharistic prayers – that all early forms originally possessed a tripartite structure, comprising two thanksgivings and a petition, and that this can be seen to underlie all later texts. His

---

11 See below, p. 135.
12 See above, pp. 75 and 104–5.

contention is as difficult to sustain as is Giraudo's theory of an original bipartite structure,[13] and Mazza has to exercise considerable ingenuity to force all ancient extant forms to fit within this particular framework.[14] Both scholars adopt far too rigid a straitjacket into which to try to insert the wide variety of Christian prayers that exist and they presume far too direct a line of descent from Jewish roots to much later texts.

The *Acts of John*

This apocryphal work is usually dated in the late second or early third century, and commonly thought to have originated in Syria. It contains two different prayers supposedly spoken by the apostle John, each at a Eucharist involving bread alone:

> We glorify thy name that converteth us from error and pitiless deceit; we glorify thee who hast shown before our eyes what we have seen; we testify to thy goodness, in various ways appearing; we praise thy gracious name, O Lord, <which> has convicted those that are convicted by thee; we thank thee, Lord Jesus Christ, that we confide in <. . .>, which is unchanging; we thank thee who hadst need <. . .> of (our) nature that is being saved; we thank thee that hast given us this unwavering <faith> that thou alone art <God> both now and for ever; we thy servants, that are assembled and gathered with (good) cause, give thanks to thee, O holy one.

> What praise or what offering or what thanksgiving shall we name as we break this bread, but thee alone, Jesu. We glorify thy name of Father which was spoken by thee; we glorify thy name of Son which was spoken by thee. We glorify thine entering of the door; we glorify thy Resurrection that is shown us through thee; we glorify thy Way; we glorify thy Seed, the Word, Grace, Faith, the Salt, the inexpressible Pearl, the Treasure, the Plough; the Net, the Greatness, the Diadem, him that for our sakes was called the Son of Man, the truth, repose, knowledge, power, commandment, confidence, liberty and refuge in thee. For thou alone, O Lord, are

---

13 See above, p. 11, n. 30.
14 See my critique of his efforts to regard the eucharistic prayer of the *Apostolic Tradition* as having developed out of the tripartite pattern of the *Birkat ha-mazon* via a form such as is found in *Didache* 10: 'The Evolution of Early Anaphoras', in Bradshaw (ed.), *Essays on Early Eastern Eucharistic Prayers*, pp. 12–13.

the root of immortality and the fount of incorruption and the seat of the aeons, who art called all these things on our account, that calling on thee through them we may know thy greatness, which at the present is invisible to us, but visible only to the pure as it is portrayed in thy man only.[15]

There are clearly problems in regarding these as typical of eucharistic prayers of the period. Not only are they literary forms rather than liturgical texts as such, but they also occur in a document that belongs to a group that was in all likelihood on the margins of Christianity rather than part of the mainstream. Moreover, there is abundant evidence that eucharistic praying in early Christianity was more commonly extemporized rather than adhering closely to a fixed text.[16] Nevertheless, even if we cannot rely on the precise details of these prayers as reflective of a wider tradition, it is not unreasonable to suppose that their general structure and themes may be representative of the way in which at least some second-century Christians prayed. Indeed, some of the themes – praise of the divine name, the gift of revelation and knowledge, and (in the first) reference to the gathering of the Church – are reminiscent of elements in the prayers in *Didache* 9 and 10, although it is important to note that the structure of the prayers is quite different. They are composed exclusively of praise and do not contain any petitionary elements; they are not made up of a small number of clearly distinguishable units each with its own doxological conclusion, but rather of a quite lengthy series of short, parallel acclamations; they appear to be addressed to Christ rather than the Father; and they make no reference to food (or drink), except in the introduction to the second prayer, but focus on more abstract gifts and appear to allude to Christ's salvific acts – perhaps to the incarnation in the first and more clearly to the resurrection in the second. This suggests a quite different cultural milieu for their origin than that of the *Didache* texts.

The roots of the epiclesis

We have seen in an earlier chapter that Justin apparently understands eucharistic consecration to be effected by the word, the Logos, and that Irenaeus similarly speaks in this connection of 'the word of invocation', 'the invocation of God', and of the bread and wine receiving 'the word of

---

15 *Acts of John* 85 and 109; ET from Wilhelm Schneemelcher (ed.), *New Testament Apocrypha* II (2nd edn, Cambridge, 1992), pp. 200–2.
16 See in particular the study by Bouley, *From Freedom to Formula*.

God' in order to 'become the Eucharist of Christ's body and blood'.[17] We cannot tell from such limited evidence, however, whether the prayers known to either of these writers contained an explicit invocation of the Logos, and if so, what form it might have taken, although we may wonder whether Irenaeus' comment that the Valentinian gnostic Marcus pro-tracted 'to great length the word of invocation' implied that 'orthodox' prayers were usually briefer. We have also seen that the third-century Syrian *Didascalia Apostolorum* provides evidence instead for an under-standing of consecration by the agency of the Holy Spirit when it stated that 'the Eucharist is accepted and sanctified through the Holy Spirit'.

While none of these sources themselves tells us enough to know what liturgical forms, if any, might have embodied their beliefs, it is possible that some light can be shed on this matter by the apocryphal *Acts of Thomas* (third-century, probably from East Syria), in spite of the critical problems and difficulties of interpretation presented by this work.[18] Scattered throughout its narrative are quite a number of prayers of very diverse kinds, including some that are made up of a series of short acclamations of praise and others that are entirely petitionary in charac-ter. One, used at a baptismal anointing, is addressed directly to the oil itself,[19] while another, used at a bread-only Eucharist, is worded thus:

> <Bread> of life, those who eat of which remain incorruptible; bread which fills hungry souls with its blessing – thou art the one <thought worthy> to receive a gift, that thou mayest become for us forgiveness of sins, and they who eat it become immortal. We name over thee the name of the mother of the ineffable mystery of the hidden dominions and powers, we name <over thee the name of Jesus>.

Before the bread is then distributed, a further petition is made: 'Let the power of blessing come and <settle upon the bread>, that all the souls which partake of it may be washed of their sins!'[20] At a Eucharist at

---

17 See above, pp. 91–4.
18 For editions of the text and a brief discussion of some of the problems associated with it, see Bradshaw, *The Search for the Origins of Christian Worship*, p. 107.
19 'Holy oil given to us for sanctification, hidden mystery in which the Cross was shown to us, thou are the straightener of the <crooked> limbs; thou are the humbler of hard works; thou art he who shows the hidden treasures; thou art the shoot of goodness. Let thy power come . . .' (*Acts of Thomas* 121; ET from Schneemelcher (ed.), *New Testament Apocrypha* II, p. 388). See also a similar type of prayer in *Acts of Thomas* 157.
20 *Acts of Thomas* 133; ET from Schneemelcher (ed.), *New Testament Apocrypha* II, pp. 391–2.

which both bread and cup are used, this prayer occurs: 'Thy holy body which was crucified for us we eat, and thy blood which was poured out for us for salvation we drink. Let thy body, then, become for us salvation, and thy blood for remission of sins. . . .'[21]

It is difficult to know which, if any, of these many kinds of prayer may have had wider currency, but among the diversity are ones in chapters 27 and 50, the former from a baptism, the latter from a bread-only Eucharist, that are the only two in the whole work to be addressed to the Holy Spirit. They both consist of a repeated series of short invocations. The prayer at the Eucharist begins as follows: '<Come gift of the Most High; S> Come, perfect compassion; Come fellowship of the male; <Come, Holy Spirit: S>' and after more invocations, it ends: 'Come and partake with us in this Eucharist which we celebrate in thy name, and in this love-feast in which we are gathered together at thy call.'[22] What is their source? Such direct invocations for the deity to be present are not characteristic of Jewish prayers from this period nor of Graeco-Roman prayers. Caroline Johnson has argued that their closest parallel lies in the magic spells of the ancient Mediterranean world,[23] and she may well be right in seeing that tradition as having influenced the development of these particular repetitive forms of invocation. However, the most likely antecedent for an early Christian use of a direct invocation in general within a eucharistic celebration seems to be the Aramaic acclamation *marana tha*, 'Our Lord, come!', found in 1 Corinthians 16.22 and also in *Didache* 10.6, and in Greek in Revelation 22.20.

Admittedly, this is a very small number of extant examples on which to predicate widespread usage in primitive Christianity, but the diverse provenance of the three texts in which it occurs does strengthen such a supposition. Even though in the *Didache* it is found in conjunction with a eucharistic meal, but not actually within the meal-prayers themselves, the other two examples do not suggest a specifically eucharistic context for its original use. It seems to have been a more general eschatological entreaty for the return of the risen Lord, which might have been a feature of early Christian gatherings, eucharistic and non-eucharistic alike. As the expectation of an imminent *parousia* began to decline

---

21 *Acts of Thomas* 158; ET from Schneemelcher (ed.), *New Testament Apocrypha* II, p. 401.

22 *Acts of Thomas* 50; ET from Schneemelcher (ed.), *New Testament Apocrypha* II, pp. 359–60.

23 'Ritual Epicleses in the Greek *Acts of Thomas*', in François Bovon, Ann Graham Brock and Christopher R. Matthews (eds), *The Apocryphal Acts of the Apostles: Harvard Divinity School Studies* (Cambridge, MA, 1999), pp. 171–204.

within Christian traditions, however, it would not have been unnatural for the invocation to have been interpreted instead by some as a call for Christ to be present at the act of worship and used in some places either outside the eucharistic prayers, as we find in the *Didache*, or as part of the petitionary element of the prayer itself, as we find in the *Acts of Thomas*. That here and in the *Didascalia* the appeal is to the Spirit rather than the Logos should not surprise us, since clear differentiation of roles had not yet been reached in the evolving doctrine of the triune God. Moreover, the close association between the two seems to be reinforced in chapter 27 of the *Acts of Thomas* where the Holy Spirit appears to be addressed as 'the name of the Messiah' in one of its invocations, or perhaps the prayer is to be understood as being addressed to both Christ and the Spirit, while in both prayers the Spirit is called 'the fellowship of the male', possibly another reference to the unity of the Spirit with Christ.

Much of the credit for analysing these particular texts must go to Gabriele Winkler, but she has taken the study of the epiclesis still further. Building upon work done by Sebastian Brock,[24] she has argued that in the earliest Syrian tradition the customary form of the epiclesis was an imperative, 'Come', addressed to the Messiah and/or his Spirit, although she later modified this conclusion slightly to claim that the very oldest form was addressed to 'the name of the Messiah', by which the Spirit was always meant. Other forms of epiclesis addressed either to Christ, such as 'may the spirit of holiness come and dwell', or to the Father, such as 'may the Spirit come and rest and abide', or imperatives addressed to the Father, as in 'Send your Holy Spirit', or petitions to the Father to send the Spirit reflected later stages of development. Perhaps more controversially, she also claimed that both epiclesis and Sanctus first emerged in Christian usage within Syrian initiatory rites, forming part of prayers for the consecration of oil and water, and then together migrated from there to eucharistic prayers.[25] This contrasts with the more common assumption that the Sanctus was adopted in eucharistic

---

24 'The Epiklesis in the Antiochene Baptismal Ordines', in *Symposium Syriacum 1972* (Rome, 1974), pp.183–218.

25 'Nochmals zu den Anfängen der Epiklese und des Sanctus im Eucharistischen Hochgebet', *Theologische Quartalschrift* 74 (1994), pp. 214–31, esp. 216–19; 'Further Observations in Connection with the Early Form of the Epiklesis', in *Le sacrement de l'initiation* (Antelias, Lebanon, 1996), pp. 66–80; 'Weitere Beobachtungen zur frühen Epiklese (den Doxologien und dem Sanctus). Über die Bedeutung der Apokryphen für die Erforschung der Entwicklung der Riten', *Oriens Christianus* 80 (1996), pp. 177–200; *Das Sanctus. Über den Ursprung und die Anfänge des Sanctus und sein Fortwirken* (Rome, 2002).

prayers from prior use within patterns of daily prayer that were modelled after Jewish practice, where the equivalent of the Sanctus is thought to have been a part of morning prayer.[26]

Attractive as Winkler's hypothesis is, it needs to be qualified in at least two respects. First, there may not have been a single original form of epiclesis. If we take into account the complete range of early epicletic material in the apocryphal scriptures, it includes invocations addressed not only to the Spirit and to Christ but also directly to the heavenly counterparts of earthly elements, as for example to 'waters from the living waters' in *Acts of Thomas* 52 and to oil in chapter 121. This implies that a much wider primitive diversity of imperative epicleses may only gradually have narrowed down to those found in later liturgical texts. Second, the baptismal context may not have been the ultimate source of the Sanctus or the epiclesis. It is at least possible that both of these were already standard prayer units in the tradition, and in separate but parallel developments then became part both of the consecration of baptismal oil and water and of eucharistic prayers at around the same time, rather than moving from the one to the other. What is important to note, however, is her more recent claim that in certain cases the whole Sanctus unit (pre-Sanctus material and Sanctus) may not be a later interpolation into already existing eucharistic prayers, as it is in other instances, but rather part of the core contents of those particular prayers.[27] This opens up what looks like a very fruitful avenue of research into the way that some eucharistic prayers were constructed.

The Anaphora of Addai and Mari

There are two later eucharistic prayers that are often claimed as having roots as early as the third century or even before and thus able to tell us what at least some eucharistic praying of the period was like. One of these is the Anaphora of Addai and Mari. Although all the extant manu-

---

26 For a review of Winkler's work and a summary of the important prior studies of the origins of the Sanctus by Bryan Spinks and Robert Taft, see Maxwell E. Johnson, 'The Origins of the Anaphoral Sanctus and Epiclesis Revisited: The Contribution of Gabriele Winkler', in Hans-Jürgen Feulner et al. (eds), *Crossroad of Culture: Studies in Liturgy and Patristics in Honor of Gabriele Winkler* (Rome, 2000), pp. 405–42.

27 See her brief reference to this point in her address, 'On Angels, Humans, the Holy, and its Perversion: Greetings from Faust', *SL* 34 (2004), pp. 52–64, here at p. 63; and her more detailed exploration of the illumination offered on this by Ethiopian sources in her book, *Das Sanctus*, summarized in English in her essay, 'A New Witness to the Missing Institution Narrative', in Johnson and Phillips (eds), *Studia Liturgica Diversa*, pp. 117–28.

scripts of this prayer are of very late date, the comparative geographical and ecclesiastical isolation of East Syria from which it comes and the strong Semitic influence on early Christianity there have encouraged scholars to believe that parts of it may be very ancient indeed. Furthermore, unlike other early extant eucharistic prayers, it appears to have been composed in Syriac rather than Greek.[28] Its most remarkable feature, however, is that the existing text lacks an institution narrative entirely, although opinion is divided over whether it fell out in the course of its history or was never there in the first place. As most of the contents of the prayer are also found in the Third Anaphora of St Peter (or *Sharar*, as it is often called) of the Maronite rite, this has led to the conclusion that a common source must lie behind the two texts. There is, however, no clear scholarly consensus on what form that original might have taken. William Macomber attempted to reconstruct the prayer as it might have been *c.* 400, which he thought belonged to the Aramaic-speaking church centred on Edessa,[29] but that is obviously very much later than the period with which we are concerned. Bryan Spinks even questions whether there ever was a single original written form, and suggests that it may be more accurate to speak simply of common oral tradition shared by the two prayers.[30] While the strongly Jewish character of much of the material in the prayer might seem to support the contention that the text does have a very early origin, it needs to be remembered that material of a similar Jewish kind also turns up in the late-fourth-century *Apostolic Constitutions*, Book 7, and scholars are not convinced that it all goes back to the earliest days of Christianity, but some believe could have developed among Christian groups continuing to use this liturgical idiom at a much later date.[31]

The difficulty of arriving at an agreed ancient core obviously creates problems for attempts to employ this prayer in order to reconstruct the early history of eucharistic prayers. Nevertheless, behind the text in its

---

28 For a critical edition, see William Macomber, 'The oldest known text of the Anaphora of the Apostles Addai and Mari', *OCP* 31 (1966), pp. 335–71; for an ET of the text and bibliography of secondary literature, see Bryan D. Spinks (ed.), *Addai and Mari – The Anaphora of the Apostles: A Text for Students* (Nottingham, 1980); and Anthony Gelston, *The Eucharistic Prayer of Addai and Mari* (Oxford, 1992).
29 'The Ancient Form of the Anaphora of the Apostles', in *East of Byzantium: Syria and Armenia in the Formative Period* (Washington, DC, 1982), pp. 73–88.
30 See his review of scholarship, 'The Quest for the "Original Form" of the Anaphora of the Apostles Addai and Mari', in idem, *Worship: Prayers from the East* (Washington, DC, 1993), pp. 1–20.
31 See David A. Fiensy, *Prayers Alleged to be Jewish: An Examination of the Constitutiones Apostolorum* (Chico, CA, 1985).

present state there does seem to be a structure composed of a number of short and clearly definable sections:

A. Introductory dialogue
B. Praise of the name of God who created and redeemed
C. Reference to the worship of the heavenly host, leading into the Sanctus
D. Thanksgiving for grace and redemption, with doxology
E. Remembrance of the fathers in the body and blood of Christ offered on the altar
F. 'That all the inhabitants of the earth may know that you alone are God. . . .'
G. Commemoration of Christ (with possible allusion to an institution narrative)
H. Epiclesis
I. Doxology

Even if some of this is of a very early date, there is little by way of objective criteria to determine which parts might belong to an ancient core and which might be later amplifications, and hence judgements have usually been made on the basis of a priori suppositions. Thus, those scholars who believe that the prayer did once include an institution narrative tend to regard section G (and an institution narrative to which it formed the anamnesis) as part of the earliest stratum, while those who do not hold this view usually exclude it. Similarly, those who regard the Sanctus and/or epiclesis as having been late additions to eucharistic prayers have tended to exclude sections C and/or H from their reconstruction of the primitive core. Those who believe that early Jewish-Christian prayers would have adhered to a threefold pattern as in the *Birkat ha-mazon* and *Didache* 10 have tended to select sections B, D, and a third unit made up of one or more of E, F, G, and H (together with the final doxology, I) as constituting the oldest elements in the prayer, though not with all their present wording. Bryan Spinks, on the other hand, has followed Jacob Vellian in proposing that the prayer was originally modelled on the bipartite structure of the Jewish morning prayers said before the *Shema* rather than the tripartite structure of the grace after meals, with the doxologies in D and I marking the end of each major unit.[32]

Spinks' suggestion has the merit of explaining how the Sanctus came to

---

32 'The Original Form of the Anaphora of the Apostles: A Suggestion in the Light of Maronite *Sharar*', *EL* 91 (1977), pp. 146–61 = idem, *Worship: Prayers from the East*, pp. 21–36.

be a part of the prayer, but suffers from a lack of hard evidence for the presence of that element in Jewish morning prayer itself at an early date. While he is likely to be correct in seeing the prayer as now divided into two major sections, each with its own doxology, it needs to be noted that the first half contains two quite distinct sub-units, B and D; and B may have had its own doxological conclusion prior to the insertion of C, if that section is indeed a later addition. Both B and D do appear to have primitive characteristics, but what, if anything, might have originally followed D is much less obvious, as that part of the prayer seems to have undergone much more revision and expansion. A few phrases in E and F appear to have a primitive ring about them, as does much of H, even if the present form of the epiclesis itself, 'may your Holy Spirit come and rest upon this oblation', represents a somewhat later development. However, even if they are ancient in origin, all these may not belong to the earliest text of this specific prayer. In particular, apart from the request in E, 'grant us your tranquillity and your peace all the days of the world' (which does not appear at all in the parallel in *Sharar*), neither E nor F is petitionary as such, and F again has a very different construction in *Sharar*.

Even if we are correct in discerning an earlier tripartite pattern behind the prayer, its content and focus are quite unlike the *Birkat ha-mazon* or *Didache* 9 or 10, with which it may be thought to share a common outline structure. In contrast to those prayers, the praise and thanksgiving centre more on redemption and make no mention at all of food and drink, the only explicit references to the Eucharist occurring in parts of the prayer that seem to be later additions. Nor does what is probably the third unit pray for the gathering of the Church, but instead H asks for 'the pardon of debts and the forgiveness of sins . . . resurrection from the dead and a new life in the kingdom of heaven'. It is therefore pursuing a quite different theological trajectory.

The Strasbourg Papyrus

The other text commonly cited as providing clues to the form of early eucharistic prayers is the manuscript catalogued as Strasbourg Papyrus 254:

> to bless (you) . . . (night) and day . . . (you who made) heaven (and) all that is in (it, the earth and what is on earth,) seas and rivers and (all that is) in (them); (you) who made man (according to your) own image and likeness. You made everything through your wisdom, the light (of?) your true Son, our Lord and Saviour Jesus Christ.

Giving thanks through him to you with him and the Holy Spirit, we offer the reasonable sacrifice and this bloodless service, which all the nations offer you, 'from sunrise to sunset', from south to north, (for) your 'name is great among all the nations, and in every place incense is offered to your holy name and a pure sacrifice'.

Over this sacrifice and offering we pray and beseech you, remember your holy and only catholic Church, all your peoples and all your flocks. Provide the peace which is from heaven in all our hearts, and grant us also the peace of this life. The . . . of the land peaceful things towards us, and towards your (holy) name, the prefect of the province, the army, the princes, councils . . . [*About one-third of a page is lacking here, and what survives is in places too fragmentary to be restored.*] (for seedtime and) harvest . . . preserve, for the poor of (your) people, for all of us who call upon (your) name, for all who hope in you. Give rest to the souls of those who have fallen asleep; remember those of whom we make mention today, both those whose names we say (and) whose we do not say . . . (Remember) our orthodox fathers and bishops every-where; and grant us to have a part and lot with the fair . . . of your holy prophets, apostles, and martyrs. Receive(?) (through) their entreaties (these prayers); grant them through our Lord, through whom be glory to you to the ages of ages.[33]

The manuscript as such dates from the fourth or fifth century and by verbal parallels reveals itself to be an early version of the Egyptian Anaphora of St Mark. The major controversy that has surrounded the text is whether what survives was a complete eucharistic prayer or just a part of something that was really much longer. The consensus is that the prayer was more or less coterminous with the extant material, and that therefore it did not include such elements as the Sanctus or the narrative of institution. A few scholars, however, remain more cautiously agnostic, and regard the case as unproven.[34] If the majority are correct, does the prayer really reproduce something that was in use for the Eucharist before the end of the third century?

The text does not seem particularly eucharistic in character. Its first section blesses God for creation, but makes no explicit mention of the

---

33 ET from R. C. D. Jasper and G. J. Cuming, *Prayers of the Eucharist: Early and Reformed* (3rd edn, New York, 1987), pp. 53–4.
34 See the review of scholarship in Walter D. Ray, 'The Strasbourg Papyrus', in Bradshaw (ed.), *Essays on Early Eastern Eucharistic Prayers*, pp. 39–56.

gift of food and drink, still less of the spiritual food and drink of the Eucharist. Nor is the theme of redemption treated here, or elsewhere in the whole prayer, nor any mention made of the death of Christ. Similarly, the last part of the prayer is a substantial block of intercessions for all sorts of people, but again without any direct connection to the Eucharist, without any epiclesis or petition for the uniting of the communicants in the hope of their future gathering into the kingdom such as we find in the prayers of the *Didache*. Moreover, the material in the middle has the appearance of a secondary addition. There is widespread agreement among scholars that the phrase 'through him, to you with him and the Holy Spirit' is a later insertion, made in order to effect a smooth transition to what follows by reworking what had previously been the doxological conclusion of the first part of the prayer.[35] The phrase that links the petitionary material in the final section of the prayer to what precedes it, 'over this sacrifice and offering we pray and beseech you', also seems to have been added for a similar reason, especially as what would then have been its original opening words, 'remember your holy and only catholic Church . . .', are more like the plain beginning of the petitionary unit in *Didache* 10.5, 'Remember, Lord, your church. . . .' In addition, the citation of Malachi 1.11 itself does not suggest great antiquity, since it has become a widely accepted principle of liturgical scholarship that the substantial quotation of biblical passages tends to be the mark of later compositions: earlier prayers instead generally allude more indirectly to scriptural texts.[36] This implies that the original core of the middle section may simply have been 'giving thanks, we offer the reasonable sacrifice and this bloodless service', an expression which has some interesting parallels in other prayers, as we shall see below, as well as precursors in earlier Christian literature.[37]

The Sacramentary of Sarapion

This collection of thirty prayers attributed to a mid-fourth-century bishop of Thmuis in lower Egypt includes a quite distinctive eucharistic prayer, the unusual institution narrative of which I have already quoted.[38] Maxwell Johnson has argued that behind the present form of

---

35 See Mazza, *The Origins of the Eucharistic Prayer*, p. 194; Ray, 'The Strasbourg Papyrus', p. 47.

36 This was one of Baumstark's 'liturgical laws'. See Anton Baumstark, *Comparative Liturgy* (London/Westminster, MD, 1958), p. 59.

37 For the antecedents of the phrase 'the reasonable sacrifice and this bloodless service', see above, p. 78.

38 See Table 3 above, and also p. 21.

the prayer can be discerned an older nucleus which, he says, has some interesting parallels with the Strasbourg Papyrus.[39] It would have begun with a series of praise units, for creation, for the revelation in Christ and for the gifts of life, immortality and reconciliation. There then would have followed a linking section, 'To you we offer(ed) this living sacrifice, the unbloody offering. And we implore you through this sacrifice, God of truth.' This then would have led into a substantial series of petitions. However, although the reconstructed prayer does resemble the general structure of the Strasbourg Papyrus, there are some significant differences in content: the praise is not simply for creation, which is mentioned only briefly here, but for redemption and other gifts which parallel some of the sentiments expressed in such prayers as those in the *Acts of John* and the Anaphora of Addai and Mari; the offering formula is briefer, lacking the Malachi quotation of the Strasbourg Papyrus; and though the petitions do include some intercession for the departed, they focus primarily on the needs of the communicants, in contrast to the wide-ranging prayers for others in the Strasbourg text. The regular inclusion of prayer for the departed that we find in Sarapion's text, rather than just for the communicants, is an easily understood development if, as appears to be the case, the Eucharist was frequently being celebrated at funerals and on the anniversaries of the death of Christians. We have already encountered in Cyprian[40] the practice of explicitly naming the departed in prayer on such occasions, and this naming is also referred to both here in Sarapion (in a rubric within the prayer) and in the Strasbourg Papyrus ('remember those of whom we make mention today, both those whose names we say (and) whose we do not say').

As Maxwell Johnson has suggested, this early version of the eucharistic prayer of Sarapion appears to have been subsequently enlarged by the addition of two other blocks of material – the Sanctus and a simple epiclesis ('Fill also this sacrifice with your power and your participation'), which were probably already features of other eucharistic prayers of the time and were now copied here, and the institution narrative and an epiclesis of the Logos ('Let your holy Word, God of truth, come upon this bread . . .') that seem to have come from a tradition related to the *Didache*, as we saw earlier in this chapter. Although this is the very first extant instance of an epiclesis of the Logos in a eucharistic text as such, that does not mean that it must have been a recent innovation. I have already noted that some second-century writers saw the Logos as the

39 See Johnson, *The Prayers of Sarapion of Thmuis*, pp. 255–9 and 271–6.
40 *Ep.* 1.2; see above, p. 114.

agent of consecration, and Johnson lists further references of this kind among third-century sources that imply that some sort of Logos epiclesis was already well established.[41] Indeed, in the light of the suggestion made earlier that the ultimate roots of the epiclesis are to be found in the eschatological acclamation *marana tha*, which appears in *Didache* 10.6, it would not seem surprising to find a Logos epiclesis in conjunction with material that stems from that particular tradition. I also claimed in Chapter 1 that the insertion of the institution narrative into the prayer was parenthetical and made for catechetical purposes, to offer an elucidation of the liturgical action being celebrated. Its migration to the prayer can be explained as a consequence of the breakdown of the catechetical system in the fourth century: those who had been baptized seemed not to have absorbed fully what Christianity was all about and what conduct was expected of them at eucharistic assemblies, and hence the liturgy needed to become itself a catechetical tool, part of which involved the regular repetition of the narrative within the rite with anamnetic intent.[42]

The *Apostolic Tradition* of Hippolytus

As I have already remarked several times, the date, provenance and stages of composition of this church order are in considerable doubt. There are also some indications that the eucharistic prayer may be a late addition to document, though that does not of itself mean that the prayer was a late composition. It could have existed for some time independently of the rest of the church order. However, while it has long been recognized that the prayer contains some elements that suggest a very early date of composition, as for example references to Jesus as the 'child' of God and the 'angel' of God's will, there are other features that point instead to a later time, as for example the appearance it gives of a seamless whole flowing continuously from initial dialogue to final doxology, as well as the inclusion of a full institution narrative and developed epiclesis. All this suggests the conclusion that, though there may be an ancient core to the prayer, in its present form it has been subject to some expansion and modification.

If we eliminate from the prayer what appear to be the later additions – the institution narrative, its accompanying anamnesis formula ('remembering therefore his death and resurrection') and the epiclesis ('and we ask that you would send your Holy Spirit on the oblation of

41 *The Prayers of Sarapion of Thmuis*, pp. 233–53.
42 See further below, p. 140.

[your] holy church') – what remains is a substantial hymn of praise for redemption, a brief offering/thanksgiving formula ('we offer to you the bread and cup, giving thanks to you because you have held us worthy to stand before you and minister to you'), a short petition for the communicants ('gathering into one, you will give to all who partake of the holy things [to partake] in the fullness of the Holy Spirit, for the strengthening of faith in truth') and a concluding doxology. This displays an interesting similarity of structure – though not content – with both the Strasbourg Papyrus and also Maxwell Johnson's reconstruction of an earlier form of the eucharistic prayer of Sarapion: a substantial praise section (though telling the story of the salvific acts of Christ much more extensively than Sarapion), a brief offering formula, and some sort of petition for the communicants (though not wide-ranging intercessions here) with final doxology.[43] The offering formula, in combining oblation with thanksgiving, particularly parallels that in the Strasbourg Papyrus, 'giving thanks, we offer', although here what is offered is explicitly bread and cup rather than the sacrifice of praise – our earliest extant liturgical text to give voice to that theological concept.

Conclusion

What this review of the early evidence for eucharistic prayers shows is that there is no clear link between what is presumed to have been the Jewish grace after meals and later Christian eucharistic texts, beyond the simple fact that both give praise and thanks and make some sort of petition. There is evidence for prayers of a strongly Jewish kind in the development of the pattern found in the *Didache* and also apparently lying behind the Anaphora of Addai and Mari, but they show no obvious literary connection with what emerge as the Jewish forms and they do not persist as the mainstream Christian practice. In their place other early Christian traditions seem to have evolved either simple prayers of praise and thanksgiving for what God had given, as is suggested by those in the *Acts of John*, or prayers that also involved some sort of invocation of the Logos or of the Holy Spirit or other petitionary element. The structural similarities between the Strasbourg Papyrus and seemingly earlier forms of the eucharistic prayers of Sarapion and of the *Apostolic Tradition* imply that one particularly prevalent form, at least from early in the fourth century onwards if not before, was the combination of praise and petitionary units by means of an 'offering' or

---

43 For a fuller development of the argument of these two paragraphs, see Bradshaw, Johnson and Phillips, *The Apostolic Tradition*, pp. 37–48.

'thanksgiving/offering' formula linking them together. As we shall see from our fourth-century witnesses in the final chapter, prayers of this kind also seem to form the basis for some others that were in use at that period.

Nevertheless, the Strasbourg prayer stands out somewhat from the other two, and indeed from all other examples of eucharistic prayers we have looked at so far. I have already remarked that there seems nothing particularly eucharistic about its contents. An exclusive focus in its praise section on creation rather than also including redemption, and yet without reference to the gifts of bread and wine, has been defended on the grounds that this was one of the hallmarks of the Alexandrian tradition – though since that tradition is largely represented by what appear to be later descendants of the Strasbourg Papyrus, that argument has an element of circularity about it. But the extensive intercession for a wide range of people, rather than just an invocation of the Logos or Spirit and/or petition for the communicants, goes far beyond anything we have yet encountered, although it does provide a precedent that others will apparently later follow. Moreover, one might have expected that a text that supposedly originated and was used for a considerable period of time within the context of the Eucharist would have picked up rather more obvious eucharistic themes and references. This, therefore, raises the possibility that what we have here is a general prayer of praise for creation and of intercession that had previously been used in a non-eucharistic context, as for example the hours of daily prayer, and was only later taken over into eucharistic usage by the insertion of its middle section with offering formula and Malachi quotation, this being perhaps a somewhat clumsy attempt to imitate the style of prayer lying behind Sarapion.

Such a development most likely happened when the Church found itself needing to provide something more substantial than the short and simple domestic formulae of earlier times, as congregations grew in size and were housed in more formal settings than hitherto. Although some local churches may have experienced such a development in the course of the third century, it would have become a more widespread and pressing need in the new surroundings of the fourth century. At that time those responsible for leading prayer are likely either to have tried to supplement the meagre prayers of earlier ages with additional material copied from elsewhere,[44] or to have cast around for what they regarded as more suitable models already in existence, regardless of whether these

---

44 As seems to have been the case, for example, with the Anaphora of the Twelve Apostles: see below, p. 150.

originally belonged to eucharistic or non-eucharistic contexts, and also to have discarded other traditional forms that did not meet contemporary needs. There is nothing in this particular prayer, therefore, that would lead one necessarily to date its introduction into eucharistic usage before the early fourth century, and hence we must beware of treating it as a trustworthy guide to what older forms of eucharistic praying might have been like.

Chapter 8

The Transformation of the Eucharist in the Fourth Century

Virtually all our substantial sources for the pattern and practice of the Eucharist in the fourth century date only from the second half of the century, and thus leave a gap of a hundred years or more from the time of Cyprian, our previous major witness. In that intervening period Christianity had undergone major changes. Christians were no longer subject to persecution, but were now followers of a legitimate and respectable religion, a *cultus publicus* that sought the divine favour in order to secure the well-being of the state. So it needed to have more of the appearance of other contemporary religions – temples, altars, a visible priesthood, and so on – and its worship therefore took on more of the features of the worship of other religions. Its number grew, and so it occupied larger and grander buildings than before, and consequently its worship became more formal in style and incorporated ritual and symbols from the civic world around to suit this new setting. Moreover, because many of the new converts were by no means as well instructed in the Christian faith or as deeply committed as most of its former adherents had been, their behaviour during church services often left much to be desired. Although, like most preachers, John Chrysostom (*c.* 347–407 CE) may have been inclined to exaggerate the extent of their irreverent conduct, there was surely some basis in reality when he accused members of the congregation in Constantinople of roaming around during the services (*In Matt. hom.* 19.7–9); of either ignoring the preacher (ibid. 32/33.6) or pushing and shoving to get nearer to hear him (*In Ioh. hom.* 3.1; see also Sozomen, *Hist. eccl.* 8.5.2; Socrates, *Hist. eccl.* 6.5.5), when not bored or downright exasperated with him (*De sacerdotio* 5.8); of talking, especially during readings,[1] and of leaving before the service was over.[2] The women caused distractions by the way

---

1 Origen had earlier made the same complaint: *Hom. in Gen.* 10.1; *Hom. in Exod.* 12.2.
2 Also evident in Antioch: see Chrysostom, *De baptismo Christi* 4.1.

they decked themselves in finery, make-up and jewellery (*In Matt. hom.* 73/74.3); young people spent their time laughing, joking and talking (*In Act. hom.* 24.4); and the behaviour between the sexes was apparently so bad that Chrysostom claimed that a wall was needed to keep men and women apart (*In Matt. hom.* 73/74.3).[3] All of these factors had a profound effect upon the form and nature of the eucharistic celebration in church, although the apparently common practice of also celebrating the Eucharist in private homes was perhaps a residual memory of its former domestic setting.[4]

Liturgy as catechesis

First of all, the eucharistic liturgy was required to supply an element of catechesis – to try to communicate the true meaning of what was going on and to impress upon the worshippers the majesty and transcendence of God, the divinity of Christ, and the sense of awe that was the appropriate response in his presence in the eucharistic mystery, as well as the sort of conduct that was called for in their daily lives.

I have already suggested in the previous chapter that the gradual introduction of the institution narrative into eucharistic prayers themselves, which we can see happening in the latter half of the fourth century, was motivated by a desire to remind worshippers of the grounds and meaning of the liturgical rite being celebrated. The Sacramentary of Sarapion and the so-called *Apostolic Tradition* are probably the oldest extant instances of this development. While there has been some debate as to whether the eucharistic prayer in use at Jerusalem at the time of writing of the *Mystagogical Catecheses* might have included the narrative, the consensus appears to be that it did not, nor did the prayer known to Theodore of Mopsuestia (*c.* 350–428 CE), thus implying that the practice was still something of a novelty.[5] But there are

---

3 I owe all these references to Robert F. Taft, '"Eastern Presuppositions" and Western Liturgical Renewal', *Antiphon* 5 (2000), pp. 10–22, here at p. 14.

4 For the evidence for domestic eucharistic celebrations at this time, see Robert F. Taft, 'The Frequency of the Eucharist Throughout History', in Mary Collins and David Power (eds), *Can We Always Celebrate the Eucharist?* (= *Concilium* 152; Edinburgh/New York, 1982), pp. 13–24, esp. p. 14 = Robert F. Taft, *Beyond East and West: Problems in Liturgical Understanding* (Washington, DC, 1984), pp. 61–80 = Maxwell E. Johnson (ed.), *Between Memory and Hope: Readings on the Liturgical Year* (Collegeville, 2000), pp. 77–96. For a more general survey of fourth-century liturgical developments, see Bradshaw, *The Search for the Origins of Christian Worship*, ch. 10.

5 For further details of this, see Burreson, 'The Anaphora of the Mystagogical Catecheses of Cyril of Jerusalem', pp. 145–8; Mazza, *The Origins of the Eucharistic Prayer*, pp. 302–9.

also signs of other attempts to instil in the congregation the right attitude of mind. These notes were struck in preaching and teaching about the Eucharist as well as in the liturgical rites themselves. Thus Chrysostom in his homilies repeatedly speaks of the 'dreadful sacrifice', of the 'fearful moment' when the mysteries are accomplished, and of the 'terrible and awesome table' that should only be approached with fear and trembling.[6] But the language of liturgical prayer also took on a more exalted tone, apparently with a similar intent. Although it is difficult to be sure of the exact age of this part of the text, the opening address of the Egyptian version of eucharistic prayer of St Basil, for example, emphasizes the majesty and transcendence of God:

> It is fitting and right, fitting and right, truly it is fitting and right, I AM, truly Lord God, existing before the ages, reigning until the ages; you dwell on high and regard what is low; you made heaven and earth and the sea and all that is in them. Father of our Lord and God and Savior Jesus Christ, through whom you made all things visible and invisible, you sit on the throne of your glory; you are adored by every holy power. . . .[7]

In sharp contrast to this exaltation of the divine, the prayer goes on to describe the earthly worshippers as 'sinners and unworthy and wretched'.

As another illustration of the use of liturgical action as a means of fostering the appropriate attitude of mind at this period, we may cite the detailed instructions given in the *Mystagogical Catecheses* concerning the reverential gestures to be used by the newly baptized when receiving communion:

> Therefore when you approach, do not come with arms extended or with fingers spread, but making the left (hand) a throne for the right, as if it is about to welcome a king; and cupping the palm, receive Christ's body, responding *Amen*. Then having carefully

---

6 See Edmund Bishop, 'Fear and Awe attaching to the Eucharistic Service', in R. H. Connolly, *The Liturgical Homilies of Narsai* (Cambridge, 1909 = Nendeln, Liechtenstein, 1967), pp. 92–7; J. G. Davies, 'The Introduction of the Numinous into the Liturgy: An Historical Note', *SL* 8 (1971/72), pp. 216–23; Josef Jungmann, *The Place of Christ in Liturgical Prayer* (London, 1965), pp. 245–55.

7 ET from Jasper and Cuming, *Prayers of the Eucharist*, p. 70. For a discussion of the development of this eucharistic prayer, see D. Richard Stuckwisch, 'The Basilian Anaphoras', in Bradshaw (ed.), *Essays on Early Eastern Eucharistic Prayers*, pp. 109–30.

sanctified the eyes with a touch of the holy body, consume, taking heed not to drop not any of it. . . . Then after partaking of Christ's body, come also to the cup of the blood, not stretching out the hands but bowing and saying *Amen* in the manner of worship and reverence, sanctify yourself also by partaking of Christ's blood. And while the moisture is still on the lips, touching it with your hands, sanctify both the eyes and forehead and the other organs of sense. (*Mystagogical Catechesis* 5.21–2)

Similar directions were also given by Theodore of Mopsuestia:

You should come up in great fear and with much love because of the greatness of the gift – fear because of its great dignity, love because of its grace. . . . When you have received the body in your hands, you adore it. . . . With a great and sincere love you place it on your eyes, kiss it and address to it your prayers as to Christ our Lord. . . .[8]

We can see from this that not only were the eucharistic elements to be treated with great reverence when they were consumed but that they were also regarded as objects of power which could be used to confer blessing on a person's body merely by external contact. This is obviously a further development of the belief that the elements possessed apotropaic powers for those who consumed them which we have encountered in some third-century sources.[9] In a similar vein, in the sermon at the funeral of his brother Satyrus, Ambrose of Milan (*c.* 339–97 CE) relates how Satyrus once wrapped up the eucharistic bread in a cloth and fastened it round his neck for protection before casting himself into the sea when the ship on which was travelling was wrecked, and so came safely to land (*De exitu fratris* 1.43).

Non-communicating attendance

As part of their efforts to urge their congregations to attain high levels of Christian conduct, fourth-century preachers regularly warned them against coming to communion while still leading sinful lives. John Chrysostom again was particularly vigilant in this regard, frequently emphasizing the sincerity and purity of soul necessary to approach the Lord's supper and even advising those who were guilty of sin to leave the

---

8 *Baptismal Homily* 5.28; ET from *AIR*, p. 255 (2nd edn, p. 242).
9 See above, p. 113.

service before the eucharistic action itself began (see, e.g., *In Eph. hom.* 3.4). Unfortunately, however, this strategy produced an unforeseen result. The aim of preaching such as this was of course not to discourage the reception of communion, but rather to motivate worshippers towards the amendment of their daily lives. But, as so often happens, the outcome was exactly the opposite of the intentions of the preachers. Many people preferred to give up the reception of communion rather than reform their behaviour. Thus began the practice of non-communicating attendance at the Eucharist. Contrary to Chrysostom's advice, many people apparently stayed until the time for communion and then left the church. Indeed, the ecclesiastical authorities were eventually forced to accept this practice, and in the end they began to make provision in the rites at the time of the communion for a formal blessing and dismissal of non-communicants in order to encourage a more orderly departure. Theodore of Mopsuestia appears to be the first to refer to such a blessing.[10]

This development also had a significant effect upon people's understanding of the Eucharist. It made it possible for them to think of the rite as complete and effective without the need for them to participate in the reception of the bread and wine, and thus helped to further the idea that liturgy was something that the clergy did on their behalf, which ultimately did not even require their presence. We have already noted from our third-century sources a trend towards regarding the Eucharist as something done by the ordained ministry on behalf of the laity, and in the changed circumstances of the fourth century that was certainly the case. Clericalism may not have been a novelty then, but it certainly took a significant step forward. The more professionalized clergy of this period increasingly dominated public worship, and the people were content to let them do it, the pure acting for the impure, the experts for the ignorant. Even John Chrysostom's very assertion that there were some moments when there was no distinction at all between the roles of priest and people in the Eucharist is itself a tacit admission that there were other times when there most definitely was a difference:

> But there are times when the priest does not differ from those over whom he presides, such as when the awesome mysteries are to be received. . . . And in the prayers also one may see the people

---

10 *Baptismal Homily* 5.22; ET in *AIR*, p. 251 (2nd edn, p. 238). For later developments, see Robert F. Taft, 'The Inclination Prayer before Communion in the Byzantine Liturgy of St John Chrysostom: A Study in Comparative Liturgy', *EO* 3 (1986), pp. 29–60.

contributing much. . . . Again in the most awesome mysteries themselves the priest prays for the people and the people pray for the
priest, for the 'with your spirit' is nothing else but this. The [prayer]
of thanksgiving again is common, for he does not give thanks alone,
but the whole people also [do]. . . . (*In 2 Cor hom.* 18.3)

Eucharist as drama

For those who now began to receive communion only infrequently
during the year and for the rest of the time attended without communicating, the Eucharist had not only ceased to be a communal action but
was no longer even viewed as food to be eaten. Instead, it became principally an object of devotion, to be gazed on from afar. It is not surprising,
therefore, that ancient liturgical commentators began to interpret the
rite in terms of a drama that unfolded before the eyes of the spectators.
The earliest instance of this known to us occurs in the baptismal
homilies of Theodore of Mopsuestia. He envisages the whole eucharistic
liturgy, from the presentation of the bread and wine to the reception of
communion, as a ritual allegory re-enacting the events of Jesus' passion,
death, burial and resurrection. This leads him to reinterpret various
liturgical actions as representing elements and moments in that story.
So, for example, the bringing up of the bread and wine by the deacons is
no longer seen as symbolizing their offering by the people but as Christ
being led to his passion; and the deacons spreading cloths on the altar
'remind us of winding-sheets'.[11] For Theodore, the climax of the rite
obviously occurs at the invocation of the Holy Spirit during the
eucharistic prayer, since 'this is moment appointed for Christ our Lord
to rise from the dead and pour out his grace upon us all'. The bread and
wine, which have until now symbolized the dead body of Jesus, become
his risen body.[12] Finally, the breaking of the bread that follows the prayer
is seen as symbolizing Christ's sharing of himself in his various resurrection appearances so that everyone was able to come to him, just as the
communicants are now able to do.[13]

Frequency of celebration

Although by the end of the fourth century considerable numbers of
people were apparently no longer receiving communion every week,

11 *Baptismal Homily* 4.25–6; ET from *AIR*, pp. 227–8 (2nd edn, pp. 216–17).
12 5.11–12; ET from *AIR*, pp. 245–6 (2nd edn, pp. 233–4).
13 5.17–18; *AIR*, p. 249 (2nd edn, p. 236–7).

there must still have been those who were still doing so, and even some –
though we do not know how many – who were continuing to take the
sacrament home for daily consumption. As we have seen, this had been
the custom in the third century and there is evidence for its survival
until the seventh century among some laity and even later in monastic
circles.[14] Indeed, Jerome (*c.* 347–419 CE) complains about Roman
Christians who, debarred from receiving communion in church, persisted in receiving the sacrament at home (*Ep.* 49.15).

In spite of the decline in communicants, however, regular eucharistic
celebrations were growing more frequent during this period. We have
already seen from our limited third-century sources that, in addition to
the weekly Sunday celebration, the Eucharist might take place at
funerals and on the anniversaries of death, especially those of martyrs,
and in north Africa perhaps even on a daily basis during the time of persecution. Although by the end of the fourth century both Alexandria
and Rome were apparently still adhering to Sunday as the only regular
day of the week for the Eucharist, this was not the case elsewhere. In
northern Syria, Asia Minor, Constantinople and monastic traditions in
Egypt, Saturday as well as Sunday seems regularly to have included a celebration of the Eucharist.[15] I have earlier suggested[16] that in parts of the
world where Christianity retained a strongly Semitic character, respect
for the Sabbath may have been retained from early times, and possibly
even a continuing assembly on that day for a service of the word after
the Eucharist had been transferred to Sunday. Although we have no
direct evidence of this practice, it seems a more likely explanation as the
basis for the development of a full eucharistic rite on that day than that
there was a sudden resurgence of a 'Judaizing' tendency in the fourth
century.[17] On the other hand, testimony from some other places speaks

---

14 See W. H. Freestone, *The Sacrament Reserved* (London, 1917), pp. 40–4; Otto
Nussbaum, *Die Aufbewahrung der Eucharistie* (Bonn, 1979), pp. 266–74; Robert F.
Taft, 'Home Communion in the Late Antique East', in Clare Johnson (ed.), *Ars
Liturgiae: Worship, Aesthetics and Praxis: Essays in Honor of Nathan D. Mitchell*
(Chicago, 2003), pp. 1–26.
15 For references, see Taft, 'The Frequency of the Eucharist Throughout History',
pp. 14–15.
16 Above, p. 72.
17 Tertullian provides evidence that as early as the beginning of the third century
some Christians in north Africa were marking the Sabbath with the same respect as
Sunday, by standing for prayer and refraining from keeping any fast on that day, and
there is abundant testimony for the existence of services of the word on Saturdays in
the fourth century. Rordorf, *Sunday*, pp. 142–53, gives further details of all this, but
is convinced that it must be a revival rather than a continuation of ancient practice.

of eucharistic celebrations on Wednesdays, Fridays and Sundays, while at Antioch it was on Friday, Saturday and Sunday that the Eucharist was held, and seemingly on Wednesday, Friday, Saturday and Sunday in Jerusalem, at least outside Lent (provided that our sources always mean a full celebration of the Eucharist on all those days and not just the distribution of communion on some of them). In some churches in the West by the end of the century a daily Eucharist may even have been known.[18] The traditional fast days of Wednesday and Friday may seem an odd choice as the first to accommodate a full eucharistic celebration, but we need to remember that Tertullian appears to refer to the regular distribution of communion on those days, and if that were a more widespread custom, then its metamorphosis into a complete eucharistic rite may be more readily understandable. That some churches appear to have reverted during Lent to a distribution of communion alone on those days may be an indication that such a service was once the norm throughout the year.[19]

The liturgy of the word

Although the pattern of worship preceding the eucharistic action that was described by Justin Martyr – a service of readings, preaching and intercessory prayer concluded with the exchange of a kiss – had apparently become of the standard practice of all major centres of Christianity by the middle of the fourth century, if not long before, yet the details of it are still relatively sparse in the contemporary sources. There are no orders of service as such, except for that in *Apostolic Constitutions* 8, and we need to be cautious about how much the uncorroborated testimony of that material really reflects the authentic practice of even one locale, let alone about applying it more broadly to the Eastern Christianity of the period.[20] Sources become more plentiful from the fifth century onwards, but since the fourth century was a time of rapid liturgical change and development, it would be dangerous to read back that evidence uncritically into the previous century. We are chiefly confined, therefore, to mere passing allusions in various sources for the recon-

---

18 See Daniel Callam, 'The Frequency of Mass in the Latin Church ca. 400', *TS* 45 (1984), pp. 613–50.

19 See, for example, Egeria, *Peregrinatio* 27.6; ET in John Wilkinson (ed.), *Egeria's Travels* (London, 1971; 2nd edn, Warminster, 1981; 3rd edn, 1999), p. 129. The Council of Laodicea (380 CE) prohibited the celebration of the Eucharist in Lent except on Saturdays and Sundays (canon 49), and also the feasts of martyrs, except on the those same days (canon 51).

20 See Bradshaw, *The Search for the Origins of Christian Worship*, pp. 93–7.

struction of what went on in this part of the eucharistic rite in the second half of the fourth century (for the first half of the century sources are virtually non-existent). John Chrysostom is a particularly valuable witness in this regard.[21]

It seems that there was an opening greeting by the bishop, or by a presbyter presiding in his place, with a response from the congregation, before the scriptural readings began. Their number seems to have varied from place to place. At Antioch, for example, there was an Old Testament reading, a reading from the New Testament Epistles, and then the Gospel reading. Testimony from elsewhere indicates that there might only be one reading prior to the Gospel, usually from the New Testament, and some sources also speak of a psalm being sung responsorially between the readings.[22] Then came the homily, or even homilies, as there is evidence that at least in the East several presbyters might preach alongside the bishop at the same service.[23] After this, there was a substantial series of intercessions. Their form appears to have differed from place to place, but they seem often to have begun with the calling forward of various groups within the congregation who were not permitted to stay and pray with the baptized – catechumens and penitents in particular – for a prayer of blessing over them and their dismissal before the intercessory prayers of the faithful themselves took place. The prayers concluded with the exchange of the kiss of peace.

Eucharistic prayers

Whatever the true authorship of the *Mystagogical Catecheses* attributed to Cyril of Jerusalem, they provide a good indication of the structure of the eucharistic prayer in use in that city in the second half of the fourth century. After referring to the washing of the clergy's hands, the exchange of the kiss of peace and the opening dialogue of the prayer, the preacher describes its contents as follows:

---

21 See F. E. Brightman, *Liturgies Eastern and Western* (Oxford, 1896), Appendix C, pp. 470ff. for the arrangement of the order of service drawn up on the basis of Chrysostom's references; also Reiner Kaczynski, *Das Wort Gottes in Liturgie und Alltag der Gemeinden des Johannes Chrysostomos* (Freiburg, 1974); F. van de Paverd, *Zur Geschichte der Messliturgie in Antiocheia und Konstantinopel gegen Ende des vierten Jahrhunderts. Analyse der Quellen bei Johannes Chrysostomos* (Rome, 1970).
22 On the origin of this psalm in the Eucharist, see James W. McKinnon, 'The Fourth-Century Origin of the Gradual', *Early Music History* 7 (1987), pp. 91–106 = idem, *The Temple, the Church Fathers and Early Western Chant* (Aldershot, 1998), IX.
23 See, for example, Egeria, *Peregrinatio* 25.1; 26.1; 27.6–7; 42.1; 43.2; van de Paverd, *Zur Geschichte der Messliturgie*, p. 131.

After this we recall heaven and earth and sea, sun and moon, stars and all creation – both rational and irrational, both visible and invisible – angels, archangels, virtues, dominions, principalities, powers, thrones, the cherubim of many faces, in effect saying the words of David: 'Magnify the Lord with me' [Ps. 34.3]. We recall also the seraphim, whom Isaiah in the Holy Spirit saw encircling God's throne and with two wings covering their face and with two their feet and with two flying and saying: *Holy, holy, holy, Lord of Hosts.* For we utter this confession of God handed down to us from the seraphim for this reason, so that we may become partakers of the hymn with the heavenly hosts.

Next, having sanctified ourselves with these spiritual hymns, we call on the merciful God to send the Holy Spirit on those things that are being presented, so that he may make the bread Christ's body and the wine Christ's blood; for clearly whatever the Holy Spirit touches is sanctified and transformed.

Next, after the spiritual sacrifice, the bloodless worship, has been completed, we beseech God over that sacrifice of propitiation for peace among the churches, for the right order of the world, for kings, for soldiers and allies, for those in sickness, for the afflicted, and in short we all pray and offer this sacrifice for all needing help.

Next, we recall also those who have died, first patriarchs, prophets, apostles, martyrs, so that God may receive our petition through their prayers and representations. Next, (we pray) also for the holy fathers and bishops who have already died and in short for all among us who have already died, believing that it will be the greatest help to the souls for whom the petition is offered (if it is done) while the holy and most awesome sacrifice is being presented. (*Mystagogical Catechesis* 5.6–9)

Because this is a commentary on the prayer and not a liturgical text as such, we must be careful not to assume that it quotes the prayer precisely and completely in every respect. Nevertheless, it is clear that the prayer has the same general shape as the Strasbourg Papyrus – praise for creation followed by wide-sweeping intercessions. It may even have included a similar expression of offering in the middle, as the author uses the phrase 'the spiritual sacrifice, the bloodless worship' at the point in the prayer where almost the same language occurs in the Strasbourg prayer. However, it does include features that were not part of that earlier text – the pre-Sanctus reference to the praise of heaven, the Sanctus and an epiclesis – but are found in the prayer of the Sacramentary of Sarapion, where they have been judged by Maxwell Johnson to be insertions into an earlier nucleus that was also similar in shape to the Strasbourg Papyrus.[24] It looks therefore as though all three prayers may to some extent share a common tradition.

It has been claimed that the prayer underlying the baptismal homilies of Theodore of Mopsuestia (5.2–14) is also similar to that in the *Mystagogical Catecheses*, although again as all that we have is a commentary rather than a liturgical text as such, it is difficult to be sure what the prayer itself might have or have not contained; in particular, the commentary seems to imply that very little preceded the Sanctus itself, but that a recounting of the salvific acts of Christ might have followed it, which, if true, would distinguish it from that in the *Mystagogical Catecheses*. Enrico Mazza has argued that in the homilies we can discern two stages in the evolution of the local eucharistic prayer: the older pattern received by the community, and reproduced section by section at the head of each part of the commentary, and the form as currently celebrated there, which Theodore describes in the commentary itself and which seems to differ in some significant respects from the former. Mazza finds this apparent later form similar to the Byzantine version of the Anaphora of St Basil.[25] However, his arguments are not completely convincing. He does not, for example, allow for the possibility that the preacher may simply have been commenting rather freely on a single text rather than alluding to another form known to him, or that the summaries at the head of each homily may not be from the hand of Theodore at all.[26]

Widespread though this particular pattern of eucharistic praying might have been, it was not the only one in use in the middle of the fourth century. In addition to some form of the Anaphora of Addai and Mari in East Syria[27] and the likely existence of others there and elsewhere that have left no easily discernible trace on later texts, there must at the very least have been in the East a Greek original of the Syriac Anaphora of the Twelve Apostles, and also an early form of the Anaphora of St Basil, as well as in the West yet another form of eucharistic prayer in use both at Rome and in Milan and known

---

24 See above, pp. 133–4.

25 *The Origins of the Eucharistic Prayer*, pp. 287–331.

26 See Clemens Leonhard, 'Did Theodore of Mopsuestia quote an Ancient "Ordo"?', *SL* 34 (2004), pp. 191–204. Bryan Spinks suggested that Theodore may have been attempting to make his remarks cover more than one eucharistic prayer in use in his community: 'The East Syrian Anaphora of Theodore: Reflections upon Its Sources and Theology', *EL* 103 (1989), p. 444 = idem, *Worship: Prayers from the East*, p. 49.

27 See above, p. 128–31.

to us from the *De sacramentis* commonly attributed to Ambrose of Milan.[28]

Although the Greek Anaphora of the Twelve Apostles is no longer extant, both John Fenwick and Robert Taft have convincingly argued it was originally used at Antioch and lies behind both the Syriac version of that prayer, but conflated there with elements from the Syriac version of the Anaphora of St James,[29] and also the Anaphora of St John Chrysostom, but conflated there with elements from the Byzantine version of the Anaphora of St Basil. From a comparison of the parallel material, it appears that the original Anaphora of the Apostles began with a relatively short thanksgiving for creation and redemption, which (without the obvious Trinitarian additions) has a very ancient appearance.[30] To this the Sanctus, institution narrative and anamnesis unit seem to have been somewhat crudely attached. These elements are followed not by an offering section, as in some other prayers, but by what appears to be a reprise of the thanksgiving from the opening section, leading into an epiclesis of the Holy Spirit. It is unclear whether intercessions formed part of the original form or not.[31] Taft contended that Chrysostom himself was the redactor of the eucharistic prayer that bears his name (probably between 398 and 404 when he was bishop of Constantinople), and Fenwick took the argument even further to suggest that the same ancestor lay behind the eucharistic prayer in *Apostolic Constitutions*

---

28 The authorship of this work has often been questioned since the sixteenth century. See Bradshaw, *The Search for the Origins of Christian Worship*, pp. 102–3.

29 The core of the Anaphora of St James appears to be the result of an amalgamation made in the late fourth century between the eucharistic prayer known to the author of the *Mystagogical Catecheses* and an early form of the Anaphora of St Basil: See J. R. K. Fenwick, *The Anaphoras of St Basil and St James: An Investigation into their Common Origin* (Rome, 1992); John Witvliet, 'The Anaphora of St James', in Bradshaw (ed.), *Essays on Early Eastern Eucharistic Prayers*, pp. 153–72.

30 It was probably something like this: 'It is fitting and right to adore you, to praise you, for you are God. You brought (us) from non-existence into being, and when we had fallen, you raised (us) up again, and have not ceased doing everything to lead us to heaven and to bestow on us your future kingdom. For all these things we thank you.' It is interesting to note that this apparent primitive core of the prayer contains no explicit Christological reference.

31 The possibility that the unit cited in the previous note constituted the totality of the original prayer has been suggested by a number of scholars, beginning with H. Engberding, 'Die syrische Anaphora der zwölf Apostel und ihre Paralleltexte einander gegenübergestellt und mit neuen Untersuchungen zur Urgeschichte der Chrysostomliturgie begleitet', *Oriens Christianus* 34 (1938), pp. 213–47, here at pp. 239, 241.

8.[32] He was reticent with regard to what additional source or sources might have been used in this last case, but Raphael Graves has since examined the prayer further and concluded that, while there is evidence of some use of the Anaphora of St Basil, the principal parallels lie with the compiler's own work elsewhere in the *Apostolic Constitutions* rather than with any other known prayer.[33]

The Coptic text of the Anaphora of St Basil exists only in an incomplete manuscript lacking the first third of the later prayer and dating from somewhere between 600 and 800, but has commonly been regarded as the oldest extant form of the prayer and as perhaps belonging to the first half of the fourth century.[34] It has been thought that it may have been the native Cappadocian eucharistic prayer brought by Basil when he visited Egypt *c.* 357 CE, and subsequently amplified by the saint himself into the longer form underlying the Armenian, Byzantine, and Syriac versions. However, recent study by Gabriele Winkler has cast some doubt on this hitherto widely accepted thesis, by pointing to elements in the Armenian version that may witness to an older recension than that of the Egyptian versions.[35] The general shape of the prayer, though not its precise content, has in part the appearance of a hybrid between the prayer in the *Apostolic Tradition*, the Strasbourg Papyrus and that in the Sacramentary of Sarapion – though I am not suggesting that its historical origin actually lies in such a combination. Its brief pre-Sanctus material has some limited parallels with the equivalent part of Sarapion's prayer; after the Sanctus it recounts the saving works of Christ before moving into an institution narrative and anamnesis/offering formula ('We also, remembering . . . have set forth before you your own from your own, this bread and this cup'), and then an epiclesis and prayer for the communicants, this pattern resembling that of

32 John R. K. Fenwick, *'The Missing Oblation': The Contents of the Early Antiochene Anaphora* (Nottingham, 1989); Robert F. Taft, 'The Authenticity of the Chrysostom Anaphora Revisited. Determining the Authorship of Liturgical Texts by Computer', *OCP* 56 (1990), pp. 5–51= idem, *Liturgy in Byzantium and Beyond* (London, 1995), III; idem, 'St John Chrysostom and the Byzantine Anaphora that Bears His Name', in Bradshaw (ed.), *Essays on Early Eastern Eucharistic Prayers*, pp. 195–226.
33 'The Anaphora of the Eighth Book of the Apostolic Constitutions', in Bradshaw (ed.), *Essays on Early Eastern Eucharistic Prayers*, pp.173–94.
34 Edition in J. Doresse and E. Lanne, *Un témoin archaïque de la liturgie copte de S. Basile* (Louvain, 1960); ET in Jasper and Cuming, *Prayers of the Eucharist*, pp. 67–73.
35 'Zur Erforschung orientalischer Anaphoren in liturgievergleichender Sicht II: Das Formelgut der Oratio post Sanctus und Anamnese sowie Interzessionen und die Taufbekenntnisse', in Robert F. Taft and Gabriele Winkler (eds), *Comparative Liturgy Fifty Years after Anton Baumstark (1872–1948)* (Rome, 2001), pp. 407–93.

the *Apostolic Tradition*; but it follows this with intercession for the living as well as the departed, thus being more like the Strasbourg Papyrus here than the Sacramentary of Sarapion.

The prayer quoted in the *De sacramentis* is incomplete, lacking the first part, but is obviously quite different in character from those in the East: a petition for God to make the offering 'approved, reasonable, acceptable' precedes an institution narrative; it is followed by an anamnesis formula similar to that in the *Apostolic Tradition* and the Anaphora of St Basil, 'remembering . . . we offer . . . this holy bread and this cup', together with a request for God to accept the offering at his altar on high (4.21–7).[36]

As this brief survey demonstrates, in the middle of the fourth century the practice of extemporizing the eucharistic prayer according to some local conventional outline was steadily giving way to written texts, which towards the end of the century began to be expanded by incorporating blocks of material from other prayers in use in other major centres of Christianity to produce the classic anaphoras of later times. Although it is usual for scholars to categorize these prayers according to the distinctive final shape that they achieved (Alexandrian, Antiochene, etc.), it might be more helpful to classify the earlier creations on the basis of rather different criteria, for instance, distinguishing those that in their praise focus exclusively on creation (e.g. Strasbourg Papyrus, *Mystagogical Catecheses*) from those that tell the story of the saving acts of Christ at some length (e.g. *Apostolic Tradition*, Anaphora of St Basil) or that lie somewhere in between (e.g. the Sacramentary of Sarapion); and similarly differentiating those that in their second half pray solely for the communicants (e.g. *Apostolic Tradition*) from those that intercede more generally (e.g. Strasbourg Papyrus) and from those that have combined the two elements (e.g. the Anaphora of St Basil).

Other elements of the rites

The *Mystagogical Catecheses* (5.11–20) describe the recitation of the Lord's Prayer immediately after the eucharistic prayer, followed by an invitation to communion, 'Holy things for the holy', with the congregational response, 'One is holy, one Lord, Jesus Christ', and then the singing of Ps. 34.8, 'Taste and see that the Lord is good', by a cantor before communion was received. There was also a prayer of thanksgiving after communion (ibid. 5.22). These elements are parallelled in

---

36 Latin text in Henry Chadwick (ed.), *Saint Ambrose on the Sacraments* (London, 1960), pp. 34–6; Bernard Botte (ed.), *Ambroise de Milan* (Paris, 1980), pp. 114–16.

some of the other sources. Although Theodore does not mention the Lord's Prayer, Ambrose in the West seems to allude to it (*De sacramentis* 5.24), but while both Cyril and Ambrose make no reference to the breaking of the bread, Theodore does, as well as describing a commixture of the bread and wine (*Baptismal Homily* 5.15–20), a similar invitation to communion to that which occurs in the *Mystagogical Catecheses*, and a prayer of thanksgiving after communion (*Baptismal Homily* 5.22–3, 29). Theodore is also familiar with several namings of individuals within the rite: in addition to the reading of the names 'of the living and the dead who have died believing in Christ' between the washing of hands and the beginning of the eucharistic prayer[37] and also apparently another commemoration of the living and departed towards the end of the prayer itself (as in the Strasbourg Papyrus and the Sacramentary of Sarapion), there is a further prayer after the commixture for those who had brought the bread and wine (*Baptismal Homily* 5.21). Chrysostom appears to refer to the breaking of bread, the Lord's Prayer and invitation to communion as having been elements of the pre-communion rite at Antioch.[38] Both Theodore and Ambrose in the West indicate that the words used at the administration of communion were 'The body of Christ', with the communicant's response being 'Amen' (ibid. 5.28; *De sacramentis* 4.25), and Theodore implies that the equivalent phrase for the cup was 'The blood of Christ'.

Eucharistic theology

The eucharistic prayers in use in the fourth century continued to articulate the same concepts of eucharistic sacrifice that are found in earlier centuries – that the offering was one either of praise and thanksgiving or of the bread and cup. Like the Strasbourg Papyrus, those that seem to have concentrated their praise on creation and lacked an institution narrative (*Mystagogical Catecheses*, Theodore of Mopsuestia?) do not even link this offering explicitly with the remembrance of Christ's own sacrifice, but others, such as the Anaphora of St Basil, do so, and this is a trend that is taken up by all later prayers. In contrast to these texts themselves, however, contemporary commentary on the rites tended to present a rather more advanced theology of sacrifice. Whatever Cyprian

---

37 *Baptismal Homily* 4.43; ET in *AIR*, p. 236 (2nd edn, p. 224). For the later history of these diptychs (as they were called), see Robert F. Taft, *The Diptychs* (Rome, 1991).
38 See F. van de Paverd, 'Anaphoral Intercessions, Epiclesis and Communion Rites in John Chrysostom', *OCP* 49 (1983), pp. 303–39.

may have meant in the third century by his statements that 'that priest truly functions in the place of Christ who imitates what Christ did and then offers a true and full sacrifice in the church to God the Father' and 'the Lord's passion is the sacrifice that we offer',[39] some fourth-century Christian writers unquestionably do use language that identifies the Church's sacrificial act very closely indeed with the sacrifice of Christ. Thus, for example, *Mystagogical Catechesis* 5.10 asserts that 'we offer Christ slain for our sins', and Gregory Nazianzus (*c.* 329–90) says that 'you sacrifice the Master's body and blood with bloodless knife' (*Ep.* 171). John Chrysostom, on the other hand, in one of his homilies, struggled between this way of speaking and the conviction that there was only one sacrifice of Christ, even though there were many celebrations of the Eucharist:

> Do we not offer every day? We do offer indeed, but making a remembrance of his death, and this [remembrance] is one and not many. How [is it] one and not many? Because it was offered once, just as that in the holy of holies. This is a figure (*typos*) of that [sacrifice] and the same as that. For we always offer the same, not one sheep now and tomorrow another, but always same, so that the sacrifice is one. And yet by this reasoning, since the offering is made in many places, are there many Christs? By no means, but Christ is one everywhere, being complete here and complete there, one body. As therefore, though offered in many places, he is one body and not many bodies, so also [there is] one sacrifice. He is our high priest, who offered the sacrifice that cleanses us. That we offer now also, which was then offered, which cannot be exhausted. This is done is remembrance of what was then done. For, 'Do this,' he said, 'in remembrance of me.' It is not another sacrifice, as the high priest then, but always the same that we do, or rather we perform a remembrance of a sacrifice. (*In Heb. hom.* 17.3)

Because the author of the *Mystagogical Catecheses* says that they believe 'that it will be the greatest help to the souls for whom the petition is offered (if it is done) while the holy and most awesome sacrifice is being presented' (5.9), this has often been understood as a reliable explanation as to why eucharistic prayers came to include a wide range of objects of intercession rather than just petition for the communicants: the idea of the Eucharist as a sacrifice must have led to the idea that it could be

---

39 *Ep.* 63.14, 17; see above, pp. 110–11.

offered for others, which in turn led to the introduction of intercessions into the eucharistic prayer. However, the true process of development could equally well have been the other way around, that it was the adoption for eucharistic use of prayers like the Strasbourg Papyrus, already containing a substantial block of intercessory material, that then gave rise to the idea of the Eucharist as a propitiatory sacrifice in the fourth century, and encouraged the introduction of intercessions into eucharistic prayers that had previously lacked them.

The realistic language about the bread and cup being the body and blood of Christ that was used by earlier Christian writers is also continued in fourth-century material, but once again liturgical texts themselves seem to have been more cautious about this than were writings about the Eucharist. Apart from citations of the words of Jesus at the Last Supper in the institution narratives that are now appearing in prayers, the prayer in the Sacramentary of Sarapion is the only one of the earliest group of prayers that we can be sure did incorporate such language in describing the eucharistic food and drink, and even that formulation, 'body of the Word . . . cup of truth', falls short of the stark realism of theological commentators of the period. However, alongside this usage, there are signs of a desire to find expressions that recognize a more subtle relationship between the eucharistic elements and Christ himself, and words like 'figure', 'sign', 'symbol' and 'type' make an appearance. Thus, for example, while the *Mystagogical Catecheses* can affirm quite unequivocally, 'Do not, therefore, regard the bread and the wine as mere elements, for they are (the) body and blood of Christ according to the master's own declaration' (4.6), it can also state that 'the body has been given to you in the form (*typos*) of bread, and the blood has been given to you in the form (*typos*) of wine' (4.3), and that communicants are 'to taste not bread and wine but the sign (*antitypon*) of Christ's body and blood' (5.20). Similarly, Ambrose of Milan appears to testify that the eucharistic prayer of his church spoke of the elements as being 'the figure (*figura*) of the body and blood of our Lord Jesus Christ' (*De sacramentis* 4.21) – unless he is simply adding his own theological gloss to a text that actually was more equivocal. We should not make too much of these differences in language, however. In the ancient world a sign or symbol was not thought of as being something quite different from the reality which it represented, but on the contrary was understood as participating in some way in that reality itself.

We can also see a gradual development in the theology of eucharistic consecration. While the earliest invocations of the Logos or the Spirit may have simply have asked for the divine presence upon the assembly, later texts link the invocation more directly with the eucharistic elements. Thus the first, and probably earlier, of the two epicleses in Sarapion's eucharistic prayer prays, 'Fill also this sacrifice with your power and your participation', probably meaning by the word 'sacrifice' the bread and wine. Some texts use imprecise verbs like 'bless' and 'sanctify', as in the East Syrian eucharistic prayer of Addai and Mari: 'may your Holy Spirit, Lord, come and rest on this offering of your servants, and bless and sanctify it. . . .' The Egyptian version of the Anaphora of St Basil, however, in requesting God to send the Spirit on both the assembled community and the eucharistic elements, introduces the verb 'show': 'And we, sinners and unworthy and wretched, pray you, our God, in adoration that in the good pleasure of your goodness your Holy Spirit may descend upon us and upon these gifts that have been set before you, and may sanctify them and show them as holy of holies.' Similarly, Theodore of Mopsuestia explains that the bishop entreats God 'that the Holy Spirit may come and that grace may descend from on high on to the bread and wine that have been offered, so showing us that the memorial of immortality is truly the body and blood of our Lord.'[40] Of course, whether in this case the final clause was actually in the prayer or was just Theodore's own interpretation of a far less precise invocation we cannot say. But these two examples reflect a theological shift towards what has been called an 'epiphany' understanding of consecration, in which the Spirit is invoked on the gifts in order that the presence of Christ may be revealed in them.

On the other hand, a number of other fourth-century sources use language about eucharistic consecration that suggests instead the idea of a change or conversion in the elements of bread and wine rather than a revealing of what was hidden. The second epiclesis in Sarapion's prayer, for example, asks, 'Let your holy Word, God of truth, come upon this bread, that the bread may become body of the Word, and upon this cup, that the cup may become blood of truth.' The *Mystagogical Catecheses*, as we saw above, appear to imply that the eucharistic prayer asked God 'to send the Holy Spirit on those things that are being presented, so that he may make the bread Christ's body and the wine Christ's blood' (5.7), although as this is rather highly developed language for a prayer that otherwise has quite a primitive appearance and so may be thought to be rather out of character with it, it is quite possible that the final clause is once again simply the author's own theological gloss on the actual text in use, which may have done no more than ask God to send the Spirit on the offering.

In Milan in the late fourth century we find similar language about a

---

40 *Baptismal Homily* 5.12; ET from *AIR*, p. 246 (2nd edn, p. 233).

change in the eucharistic elements in *De sacramentis*, but in contrast to the Eastern sources, the author understands this to be effected not by an invocation of the Holy Spirit (which seems to have been absent from eucharistic prayers in the West) but by the recitation of the words of Christ in the narrative of institution, which was now included in the prayer:

> How can that which is bread be Christ's body? By what words, then, is the consecration (effected), and by whose saying? (Those) of the Lord Jesus. For everything that is said before is said by the priest: praise is offered to God, prayer is made for the people, for kings, for others. When it comes to the accomplishing of the venerable sacrament, the priest does not use his own words any more, but he uses the words of Christ. Therefore, Christ's word accomplishes this sacrament. (*De sacramentis* 4.14)

This appears to be a somewhat different development of the idea that consecration is effected by the word of God and prayer, which we have earlier seen to go back at least to the Pastoral Epistles (1 Tim. 4.5), but it was the one that ultimately dominated eucharistic theology in the medieval West.

Conclusion

We have come a long way from the simple domestic rituals that seem to have constituted the historical roots of the Eucharist. By the late fourth century not only had the original meal long since been reduced to symbolic proportions but at least for some of those who were there it had now become more often something to be watched and worshipped from afar than to be consumed. Thus, there were those present at the rite who were non-communicants, and at the same time there were others who were communicants in the absence of the rite. But while the meal may have decreased in size, the prayers over the bread and cup had increased in length to become much more substantial and complex orations in the public settings in which they found themselves. Yet, for all that, their theology still remained relatively undeveloped. It was only towards the very end of the century that we see the first explicit signs appearing in these texts of the eucharistic doctrines that had already been the established beliefs of their users for a considerable period of time. So momentous were these changes and developments in theology and practice in these first few centuries that they would not be surpassed even by those that were to come in succeeding ages.

Index of References

OLD TESTAMENT

NEW TESTAMENT

LITURGICAL TEXTS

Index of Modern Authors

References to pages which provide full bibliographical details are indicated by the use of **bold** print.

Index of Subjects